The Art of Effective Piano Teaching

By

Dino P. Ascari

ISBN: 1-4033-7343-4 (e-book)
ISBN: 1-4033-7344-2 (Paperback)
ISBN: 1-4033-7345-0 (Dust Jacket)

This book is printed on acid free paper.

1stBooks - rev. 02/27/03

Acknowledgments

To My Loving Wife Debbie,
for putting up with all the long hours involved in completing this
project.

Many Thanks to Trisha Bauer,
for her valuable input and revision suggestions.

To My Mom and Dad,
for their sacrifice in giving me piano lessons when I was young.

To My Children Kristy, Dina, Michael, and Steven.

And to My Other Children, My Students.

Table of Contents

Foreword

Once a student reaches the intermediate to advanced levels of piano performance, a student's musicality is largely influenced by that of his or her teacher. At such a level and beyond, the instructor's musicianship as demonstrated by his or her ability to interpret music becomes more important than the instructor's ability to teach. However, just the opposite is true with beginning students. Beginning students are far more influenced by an instructor's ability to motivate and teach than they are by an instructor's own musicality.

Why is it that so few piano students ever reach a lasting degree of proficiency? Is talent the only factor? *The Art of Effective Piano Teaching* says, "No!" Author, Dino P. Ascari, believes that if certain motivational techniques are combined with sound teaching principles, virtually every beginning piano student can learn to play and enjoy a lifetime of musical expression. But, of course, most beginning students are taught by beginning piano teachers who may be proficient on their instrument but have little, if any, idea of how to motivate their students past the initial stages of learning. Even experienced teachers often believe deep down that the reason so many students drop out is simply because of a lack of talent.

The Art of Effective Piano Teaching targets the beginning teacher. It combines an eclectic array of sound teaching principles with new and innovative thinking. It is specific, when necessary, and at other times quite general. The reason for this is so that novice teachers (as well as experienced ones who are still teachable) will be able to provide their students with a solid educational foundation. At the same time it encourages instructors to adapt the principles and techniques to their own unique personality and teaching style.

May all teachers who read this book continue to be as excited about improving their teaching skills as they are about practicing their chosen profession.

Introduction

The focus of *The Art of Effective Piano Teaching* is to help teachers, whether novice or experienced, create an atmosphere where learning to play piano is exciting, challenging, and most of all, fun. The aim is to enable teachers to develop in students an "I can do it" attitude and thus build self-esteem by making piano a positive experience.

Teachers need only to talk with fellow professionals or read the available literature to realize that there is a plethora of views regarding the proper pedagogical emphasis to place during the initial years of piano study. Some teachers are of the opinion that beginning students must first learn to feel and understand rhythm. Other teachers believe that technique is much more important. Still others would insist that students must be submersed in theory, otherwise they will lack comprehension, lose interest, and quit. There is even a widely held school of thought that says to forget about rhythm, technique, and theory and that the only way to be a successful piano teacher these days is by teaching popular music at the expense of all else. As the methodology of this book is made clear, these pedagogical positions will be brought into proper balance, allowing teachers to make sense of this often-conflicting body of opinion.

Most teachers, even the successful ones, will have to admit that a relatively low percentage of students ever learn to play fluently. This is because the task of learning to play piano is similar in magnitude to that of rolling a boulder up the side of a huge hill. Unless one gets the boulder to the very top, it will certainly roll back down to the bottom. Too many students take years of lessons and push that boulder up the proverbial mountain, only to let it slip back down, stopping instruction before ever reaching a lasting degree of proficiency. After a while, it is as if they had never taken lessons at all. Thus, the challenge for teachers is to find ways of making the learning process exhilarating and stimulating, especially until such time as students become intrinsically motivated. When teachers succeed, their students experience a lifetime of musical enjoyment.

Although there are no absolutes in piano pedagogy, you can count on the fact that every student is different and will learn at a dissimilar pace. In this book we will look at ways of optimizing that pace and maximizing each student's potential.

The Art of Effective Piano Teaching adapts sound teaching methods to the unique personality and gifts of the individual student, techniques that can be applied to all ages, at every level of mastery. We will consider the vital role of the parent both at the lesson and at home and will examine new and innovative ways of quantizing students' progress through the use of aids such as a metronome, stopwatch, and "Student Progress Graph." We will look at motivational tools such as "Mystery Tunes," the use of praise, the running of recitals, and more.

You will add a new degree of excitement to your piano teaching career as you digest the contents of this book and see firsthand how the techniques actually work. That excitement will surely carry over to your students!

Dino P. Ascari

Chapter I-Getting Started: The First Lessons

Most experienced teachers will agree that prior to the first lesson it is wise to settle a few important issues with the parents of prospective students. Some of these issues relate to the business of teaching piano and will include the lesson fee and make-up policy. Another will relate to establishing the role of the parent at the lesson and at home.

First, teachers will need to set a fee for their services that is in keeping with their level of expertise and in line with those charged by other teachers in their area. Next, it is necessary to establish a make-up policy for missed lessons. It is also a good idea to prepare a "Student Information Sheet" for parents to fill out at the first lesson and to photocopy a "List of Required Books and Music Aids" that each beginning student will have to purchase. Topics such as lesson fees and make-up policy will be discussed in detail in a later chapter (see chapter IX).

Establishing the Role of the Parent at the Lesson and at Home

Does the parent really need to be involved? This crucial question must be addressed if teachers are to provide their students with the best possible experience at the lesson and at home. By becoming familiar with the success of the Suzuki School of Music, piano teachers may gain worthwhile insight.

When Suzuki methodology was first introduced to the western world back in 1969, critics were stunned when it was shown that students, some as young as three years of age, could perform by memory many of the world's greatest compositions with near flawless perfection. How is this accomplished? While there are a number of reasons, the most important is the way Suzukians utilize the parent in the student learning process, initially, at the lesson as an observer, and then as the "Teacher-at-Home" or practice coach. Suzuki methodology demonstrates that with the parent as part of the student-teacher team, the chances of success will greatly increase for such students.

The importance of the parent being directly and actively involved should come as no surprise. Just as few children would do their homework each day if their parents did not hold them accountable, the same holds true for practicing piano. Can parents really expect their children to succeed on an instrument if they are not willing to take an active part in assuring that practicing is done correctly and consistently? Of course not! So, before a teacher enrolls a student in music lessons, he or she must first find out if the parent is willing to make an equal commitment to that expected of the child.

At the lesson, parents will function mainly as observers. Although they can ask questions, the teacher must be the one in charge. Teachers must insist that parents do not talk for their children, because if parents continually interrupt and interject, teachers will find it almost impossible to develop an ongoing and vibrant relationship with their students.

At home, the role of the parent changes drastically. The parent becomes the teacher-at-home and must implement the instructions given at the lesson. For that reason, it is vital that both parent and student understand each assignment and feel confident that the desired goals can be achieved.

Practice time should be a time of bonding for parent and child. Yet, that will not happen unless parents have been given realistic expectations of what their child may or may not accomplish during the week. Additionally, at or prior to the first lesson, teachers and parents must discuss the overriding goal of piano lessons; that is to build a student's self-esteem by making piano a positive experience. When armed with realistic expectations and an understanding of the importance of building self-esteem, most parents will be able to focus on their primary role, that of encouragement and exhortation. Satisfactory completion of each assignment will be a natural outgrowth of a proper practice environment.

As the years of lessons go on, and students naturally become more self-sufficient, parents will notice that the need to be part of the everyday practice session will diminish. However, parents can rest assured that their years of hard work and dedication will certainly not go unrewarded since a musical bond will have been created—one that will not be easily broken.

Student Information Sheet

It is a good idea to develop a "Student Information Sheet" for parents to fill out at the first lesson. This is a great way of keeping track of important information. If teachers ever need to mail notices, memos, pamphlets, etc. to any of their students, it is nice to have quick access to their home addresses as well as their e-mail addresses. Equally important, should the unexpected come up, it is advantageous to have the parent's home and work phone numbers on hand as well as any cell phone and/or pager numbers. It is even helpful to have an alternate contact should all else fail.

Another valuable tidbit of information to have in the records is that of each student's date of birth. Teachers should make sure these dates are logged into their appointment books or computer organizers so they can wish their students an unexpected "Happy Birthday" at the appropriate time. Knowing the students' date of birth allows teachers to quickly calculate the students' age year after year and wish them the correct number birthday (i.e. a Happy 8th or 9th Birthday). Students feel special when teachers know important details!

Some teachers go as far as having a box of musical pens, pencils or notepads on hand to use as birthday gifts. You do not need to spend a great deal of money on these things. In this case, it is definitely the thought that counts.

Preparing a List of Required Books and Music Aids

Next, a list of items that will be used by the student at the lesson and at home needs to be prepared. This list will include items such as a one-subject spiral-bound notebook for assignments, a music manuscript book, method books selected to teach rhythm and note reading, a metronome, flashcards, and anything else that may be needed in the near future.

By working from a printed list, parents will be less likely to make mistakes when purchasing the necessary items. Also, a printed list sends the message that the teacher has done his or her part in making sure the student is prepared for the next lesson.

Notice in the list of suggested items the requirement for a one-subject spiral-bound notebook. We are not talking about a music notebook here but a simple lined-paper notebook as used in school. This is the notebook where the weekly assignments will be written. There is absolutely no reason to write assignments in a music manuscript book. First of all, they are more expensive than regular notebooks. Secondly, they usually have fewer pages, and also, it is more difficult to read words written over the lines of a music staff than words written on a lined page. Use music notebooks for music and regular notebooks for assignments and theory. In addition, be sure to tell well-meaning parents that in this case a one-subject notebook is superior to a two, three or even five-subject one. That is because a one-subject notebook will usually last at least one to two years and will be far less cumbersome to deal with on a weekly basis.

The First Lesson

The first lesson is probably just as scary for the beginning piano teacher as it is for the beginning student. Teachers have thirty minutes to win over students and make them feel that playing piano is doable. The teacher needs to establish a rapport with both the student and the parent and the child has to walk out of the lesson knowing more about piano than when he or she first walked in.

Before the start of the first lesson, teachers should review the student's first and last names. Nothing is more embarrassing than being unsure of or calling a student (or parent for that matter) by the wrong name. It may seem insignificant, but greeting your clients by name (along with wearing a warm smile) immediately helps them feel more comfortable and goes a long way toward easing the initial tension.

Once the introductions are done, sit the student at the piano and position yourself where you can see and talk face to face with both the parent and the student. Time to get down to business!

A good way of getting started is to discuss the ground-rules for taking lessons—ground-rules for both student and parent. Within these ground-rules lies what many consider to be the most important basis for successful piano study—the basis of honesty between student and teacher. When dealing with young students, one way of proceeding is to say, "Today, I'd like to go over the ground-rules for taking piano lessons. What do the words ground-rules mean to you?" Once the term "ground-rules" has been discussed, the teacher can go on to say, "Before we review your ground-rules, did you know that your parent has rules to abide by at the lesson, too?"

The primary reason for discussing the parent's ground-rules first is to break the ice for when it is the student's turn. I tell my students (in front of their parents) that at the lesson, "Parents should be seen and not heard." Of course, I say it in a light-hearted way—no need to start off on the wrong foot with the parent. This usually elicits a chuckle from the students and prepares them for what is to come. But what is to come?

When students take their first piano lesson, they usually expect a list of rules a mile long—rules so numerous and onerous that no one in their right mind would ever consent to taking piano. Teachers must alleviate these fears and set the tone for all future piano lessons by giving ground-rules students can live with.

The Student's Ground-Rules

1) If you do not understand what I am saying, or if you are having trouble with what I am teaching you, then you must tell me. 2) You must always give me your best.

Wow, that's it! No practicing six hours per day and missing all their favorite TV shows? Do not be surprised if you see a look of relief on their faces once they realize that these rules are the only ones you have. (The rest of your expectations can be introduced at subsequent lessons and at the appropriate times.)

At this point, the importance of rule number one must be reinforced. This can be done in a number of ways, such as painting a word picture. I usually tell my students about an experience I had way back in the first grade that has had a profound impact on my life:

Many years ago when I was in grade school, the teacher was trying to teach the class long division. As with any new concept, no one in the class wanted the teacher to know that they did not have a clue as to what she was talking about. So when the teacher asked the question, "Does everyone understand?" all she saw was head upon head, bobbing up and down, implying, "Yes, we understand."

Well they didn't understand and I didn't understand either. As the sweat started to drip down my brow, I raised my hand and said, "I'm sorry Miss White, I don't understand what you are teaching." You could see the relief on the faces of my fellow classmates. Fortunately for them, there was one kid in the class foolish enough to let the teacher think he was a real dummy—me!

So the teacher explained it again. After she was finished, she repeated the question and asked, "Does everyone now understand this concept?" Well glancing out from the corner of my eyes I could tell that no one did. But again, heads were bobbing up and down assuring the teacher that we were all on the same page. What did I do? I raised my hand, or at least tried to. My arm felt like a 200-pound lump of lead. Somehow, I managed to get it high enough so that the teacher noticed my look of dismay. After about 15 minutes of this going on, the teacher changed one key word and guess what, the whole thing clicked! By that time everyone else in the class understood the concept too, and I became the unsung hero.

The teacher said to me, "I'd like to speak with you for a moment after school." Well needless to say, my stomach was in knots for the rest of the day. When class ended, thinking that I was surely in trouble for asking all those questions, I slowly walked up to the teacher as my classmates were leaving the room. But to my surprise, instead of chastising me, just the opposite occurred. She said, "When you raised your hand to tell me that you didn't understand, I could tell from the blank looks on your classmate's faces that they didn't understand either. Therefore I want to commend you for your perseverance. Keep up the good work!"

I have never forgotten that day in class. And it made me realize that when it comes to teaching, sometimes all it takes is one different word to make a concept come to life. Therefore, students must feel comfortable that if they do not understand something, it is okay and probably not their fault. It is up to teachers to figure out ways of changing their presentation or adjusting their words so that students can understand what it is they are trying to get across. But, it works both ways, does it not? How can students expect teachers to do their jobs if they will not tell them when they are having trouble?

Some may say that this is a long story to get a simple point across. However, the point cannot be overemphasized that there must be honesty between student and teacher, right from the start. Honesty does not prevail when students allow teachers to think they understand something when they really do not!

Teaching Basics: A Review of Discovery Learning and Step-by-Step Teaching Methodology

Discovery Learning is a method of pedagogy where the teacher asks a series of questions designed to lead students to "discover" the answer for themselves. For example, suppose you want to teach a beginning student that the black keys are grouped in twos and threes on the piano. Instead of saying, "See the black keys, they come in groups of twos and threes," you can ask the following questions: "What can you tell me about the keys on the piano?" (In this case the question is purposely vague so that the teacher can get a feel for the student's perceptive abilities.) Correct answer: "They are black and white." "And what can you tell me about the black keys?" Depending upon the age and how astute the student is you may get answers anywhere from, "I don't know" to the correct answer of, "They come in groups of twos and threes."

Even if students have initial difficulty coming up with the correct response, do not give up. Ask, "Is there anything special about the black keys?" or, "Do they come in groups?" Of course, phrasing the question in this way basically gives them the answer. However, in the students' mind, they will still think that they have figured it out for themselves. Accordingly, they will feel good about their sense of accomplishment.

So, here lies the power of Discovery Learning. Whenever a connection is made between the learning process and a sense of accomplishment, concept retention is enhanced.

Another important teaching principal that goes hand in hand with Discovery Learning is that of Step-By-Step Teaching Methodology. In order to facilitate a step-by-step learning process with students, teachers must first have a clear understanding of the component parts or steps that go into arriving at the correct answer. For example, for students to fully grasp where "C" is on the piano, they must first understand 1) that there are both white and black keys on the piano, 2) the black keys come in groups of twos and threes, and 3) all Cs come just before (or to the left of) the group of two black keys.

It is easy to take for granted the complexity of what students are expected to comprehend. What is simple and second nature to us is far from simple to our students. Therefore, before teachers can help students discover a correct answer, they must make sure that they can lead them through the learning process step by step.

Pacing the Introduction of Concepts and Skills

As we explore effective ways of teaching the basics, it would be wise to keep in mind that no matter how skilled teachers become, each student will still learn at his or her own pace. This does not mean that effectual teaching will not maximize that pace. It only means that every student is unique, with different gifts, talents, and mental abilities. It is the teacher's job to unlock their students' potential and to help them learn at a pace that is not too fast and not too slow, but rather a pace that is just right for each individual.

Here is every teacher's dilemma: If they wait for students to completely master a previous concept or skill before introducing the next one, then their students will learn at a snail's pace. On the other hand, if they proceed ahead when real confusion still exists, they will lose their students emotionally and sooner or later they will want to quit. So, how does a teacher decide what the correct pace should be?

The rule of thumb for pacing the introduction of concepts and skills is this: If the next concept or skill reinforces the previous one and a sense is ascertained that the student understands what has been already taught, then it is advisable to try moving ahead. If, however, moving ahead brings the student to completely new ground or if it is sensed that mastery of any concept or skill is going to take much more time, then stop, devise appropriate drills, and make those drills the focus of that week's assignment.

We now come to an important teaching axiom: Concepts and skills must be reinforced through drills. In other words, a concept or skill can only be mastered through repetition.

Drills are designed for repetition. And through repetition, concepts and skills become internalized. But, drills can be boring. The challenge is to make them as fun and enjoyable as possible.

Think of learning piano as climbing up a huge ladder—a ladder so tall that it reaches up to the sky. Each concept or skill is one rung on that ladder. Before students can be allowed to climb up to the next rung, they must have a firm understanding and grasp of the material for the step they are on.

It is a big mistake to think that problems will clear themselves up at a later time. In fact, the opposite is true. Problems will only get worse; misconceptions and misunderstandings do not magically disappear. Just as the builder of a house knows that if the foundation is not secure the house will fall down when the winds come, the same holds true when it comes to learning a musical instrument. Therefore, the job of the teacher is to make the musical foundation secure. This can only be accomplished by using Discovery Learning techniques in a step-by-step process and by drilling each concept and skill until students can demonstrate readiness to move ahead.

Goal of the First Lessons

The goal of the first few lessons is to get students to start making music and to understand the basics. The basics include 1) learning the finger numbers, 2) developing the ability to sing and match pitches, 3) understanding the concept of up and down on the keyboard, 4) recognizing the notes on the piano, 5) reading and understanding musical notation, and 6) feeling the beat and rhythm.

Making music must go hand-in-hand with comprehending music. In other words, students must learn an appropriate amount of theory to support the level they are at. Keep in mind that "appropriate" is the operative word here. Long and involved explanations are unnecessary at this point.

Teachers must wait until their students are ready before introducing deep theoretical concepts. It is not wise to burden them with unnecessary details that cannot possibly be understood at their current level. Often, the discovery learning technique provides students with all the theory they need, especially at the beginning stages.

Learning the Finger Numbers

When introducing the concept of finger numbers, students can be asked the question, "Did you know that in music each of our fingers gets a number? This is so that we can learn to play piano easily by having certain fingers play certain notes at different times." It can then be asked, "What finger do you think will be our number one finger?" Of course, the teacher will be asking for a guess. If the student gets it right, the teacher can praise the student. If not, nothing needs to be said.

For younger students, ask them to place their right hand on the inside cover of their music manuscript book. If they do not have one yet, use a blank piece of paper and tape it in later. Now, take a pencil and draw the outline of their hand. Depending on their age, I often accompany the tracing procedure with the sound of a Choo-Choo train. Do the same for the left hand. With the outline of both thumbs facing each other on the page, ask them to write the number "1" on each thumb. Have them do the same for fingers two through five. Kids love a "hands-on" approach to music and they remember what they learn better, too!

Once all the finger numbers are written in, have them write their name and age at the top of the page (if necessary, you can help them with this). Should they ever come across this book as an adult, having their name and age at the top of the book will surely bring back fond memories of their years of taking piano lessons and will even be fun to show their children!

If students are older, there is no need for the tracing routine. All teaching methods must be age-appropriate. We can, however, tell them a little trick for remembering the finger numbers: The thumb is the number one finger and the way to remember that is to say, "Thumb rhymes with One" (at least it does in my dictionary of piano rhymes!) So, if students are ever unsure as to which finger is which number, they can always start with the thumb as the number one finger and proceed from there. In subsequent months, whenever hesitancy is sensed as to proper finger use, all the teacher has to do is have the student repeat that rhyme.

Teaching "Process"

Whenever possible, teachers should teach "process" rather than specifics. Students need to learn how to break down complex tasks into smaller, more manageable parts. Once the tasks are broken down, students will be able to proceed step by step to arrive at the correct response. Using the finger numbers as an example, let us say that a student forgets that the ring finger is the fourth finger. By knowing that the thumb is the number one finger, students have a quick and easy way of figuring out what finger number their fourth finger is. All they need to do is count up from their thumb. So, instead of memorizing five different finger numbers, they memorize one process. As the process gets faster, recognition becomes instantaneous and their understanding deepens. Comprehension comes with far less effort and is significantly more satisfying when all that has to be done is recall a process rather than distinguishing one concept from another.

As children grow up, life gets more and more complex. Tasks and responsibilities increase exponentially. So, if at a young age students learn to break down tasks and go through the process of mastering the component parts, they are really being prepared for life. To drive home this point, I often pose this hypothetical question to my students: "If you had a ton of bricks, and I asked you to move them from one spot to another, what would you do? Would you try pushing on the whole pile, hoping that somehow you could muster the strength to move them all at once? Or, would you agree that a ton of bricks could only be moved one brick at a time?"

Of course, when it comes to moving bricks it is easy for students to see that a one-at-a-time approach is the best way to get the job done. But, when it comes to music, it is not as easy for them to recognize the intricacy of the concepts and skills that they are trying to comprehend. Therefore, teachers must first help students discover the process that will lead them to the right answer and then review it as often as necessary until it becomes internalized.

Developing the Ability to Sing and Match Pitches

Many teachers underestimate the importance of pitch matching. They have bought into the belief that if students have any talent, they will naturally have this ability; and they also believe that if students cannot match pitch, there is nothing they could do about it anyway. Yet, developing the aptitude to sing and match pitches will bring lasting benefits to students.

I would agree that the students who can easily sing and match pitches are probably the more talented students. But, learning to play piano has nothing to do with talent (unless, of course, one's goal is to make it to Carnegie Hall). Virtually every student, regardless of talent, can and should experience the enjoyment that comes from making music. Learning to sing and match pitches will positively affect every area of musical development.

One such area is the ability to hear music in one's head before ever playing a note. Have you ever noticed jazz musicians when they are improvising a solo? Many times they will sing the notes that they are playing. (George Benson even records his guitar solos this way!) This is because improvisation originates in the mind and is executed through the fingers. The singing of the pitches somehow connects the two, thereby training the musical ear. Though most students may never become famous jazz musicians, all students will benefit by developing a highly trained ear for music.

In the following chapter we will be reviewing the criteria for passing pieces in the method books. One of the requirements will be to "Play and Sing the Notes." Through this criterion we will be teaching ear training at the same time we are teaching note reading. The correct singing and matching of pitches is essential to that goal.

To test students' pitch matching gifts, play middle C on the piano and ask them to sing "La." Make sure they understand that you want them to sing the same note you are playing. Continue in a likewise manner with middle D and E. (The notes will be limited to C, D and E and expanded later, if necessary, so that we can be sure that the pitches are kept in the students' vocal range.) If each note is sung properly, then no additional time and effort is required at this point. If they have trouble, then ways must be devised to develop this skill.

If a student's pitch is fairly close to that being played, but still far enough away that it cannot be called a match, then all that is likely needed is for the teacher to exhort the student to listen more carefully and try again. Most students will be able to sing on pitch if they really focus. Unfortunately, some students will remain far off key. When this happens, do not give up and assume that the student is tone deaf. Believe it or not, in all my years of teaching piano I have never come across a student who was truly tone deaf. Many have had great difficulty with the matching of pitches, but ultimately, they have been able to do it. When working with students that need remedial work in this area, I have found the "Siren" approach to be of great value.

The "Siren" approach is where the student starts singing "Ah" real low, and then raises his or her voice higher and higher until he or she hits the pitch being played—just like a siren. As the student's voice approaches the correct pitch, the teacher exhorts the student to keep the siren going. If the correct pitch is passed, the siren must be started again. When the proper pitch is matched, the teacher signals to the student to stop the siren but continue singing the note. Once on pitch, the student is encouraged to listen carefully to how his or her vocal pitch matches the pitch of the note being played.

At first, most students will either pass the proper pitch or take an excessive amount of time reaching it (if at all). However, after a few weeks of working on the siren with the teacher at the lesson and practicing it at home with the parent, even the most "tone-deaf" student will be able to match pitches with relative ease!

The Concept of Up and Down on the Keyboard

In addition to learning to match pitches, comprehending the concept of up and down on the keyboard must be tackled immediately. I have always been surprised at the number of beginning students that have difficulty in this area. One would think that if the teacher started at middle C and played successive notes going higher, most students would understand that the notes are going "up" on the piano. But, if asked the question, "Are the notes going up or down?" at least half the students will answer, "Down!" If we reverse the direction, the same thing happens.

One possible explanation for this bewilderment is that on the piano the black keys are physically higher than the white keys. Initially, many students confuse physical height with pitch height. In their mind the only way the concept of up and down makes any sense is if the notes go "up" from a white key to a black key or "down" from a black key to a white key. So, the concept of up and down on the keyboard is not as easy as it may seem. How then can this seemingly simple concept be taught?

First, students must understand that when talking about up and down on the piano we are not talking about physical height but rather the sound or pitch of the notes as they get higher or lower. Here, pitch-matching ability also comes in handy, because when students sing the notes being played, they generally have less trouble distinguishing up from down. It is almost as if they can feel their throat tightening and loosening as the pitches go higher or lower. Their voice-box seems to send a message to their brain, "These notes are getting awfully high or awfully low!"

As with any concept or skill, the recognition of up or down on the piano is a concept that needs to be reinforced. One way to do that is to assign drills or make up games where students play notes that go up or down on the keyboard. Another way is to use a pre-method book such as The Music Tree's "Time to Begin"[1] that teaches the concept of up and down through songs such as "Take-Off" and "Landing," etc.

Introducing the Notes on the Piano

When introducing the notes on the piano, part of the approach will be to incorporate the drawing of a keyboard into the student's music manuscript book. On the first page a horizontal line should be drawn across the page approximately six inches from the top. Next, fifteen vertical lines will need to be drawn for the white keys. This will yield a total of fourteen white notes.

The reason for being so specific regarding the number of keys is that we do not want students to have difficulty relating this keyboard to that of the actual piano. If fewer keys are used, a group of black keys might get truncated, thus causing confusion. The drawing will range from F all the way up to the second E and will encompass two complete sets of two and three black keys (see illustrations below).

Illustration 1: Preliminary Drawing of White Keys Without the Black Keys Added

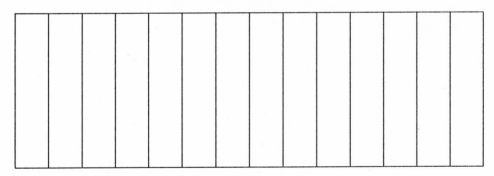

Before outlining the black keys, students can be asked, "What is wrong with this picture of the keyboard?" Most will answer, "There are no black keys!" Of course, that is correct! Without the black keys all the white keys would look the same.

---

[1] The Music Tree, by Frances Clark and Louise Goss, published by Summy-Birchard, Inc.

Now let us add in the black keys.

Illustration 2: Completed Drawing

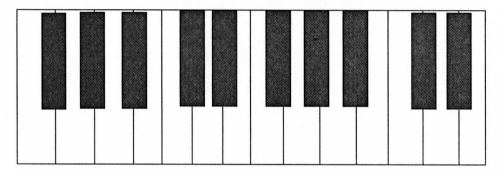

At this point some may wonder, "Why not save time and hand out a photocopy of a keyboard with the notes already labeled or show students where they can find a picture of a keyboard already printed in their method book?" The answer is simple: We want the keyboard to come alive in the student's sight. As students are led to discover the notes, they will be the ones to label the keyboard drawing in their book. And once they get to "G," they will see for themselves that there is no room left for "H." It will then be easier to understand why the musical alphabet only goes from A through G.

As outlined previously in the step-by-step teaching example, to recognize "C," students must first understand that there are both white and black keys on the piano and that the black keys are grouped in twos and threes. By diagramming the keyboard in the student's presence, most students will have no problem recognizing the fact that there are both white and black keys. If difficulty exists at this basic level, it might be wise to hold off lessons until the student is a little older. But, even if a child is piano ready, going on to the next step and being able to locate the various groups of two and three black keys quickly and easily may take quite a bit of drilling.

In order to facilitate the speedy recognition and location of the various groups of black keys, teachers can let the younger students stand as they make their way up and down the piano keyboard. Make sure the piano bench is pulled back far enough to allow them room to maneuver. If they are of sufficient age, they should be able to reach all the notes on the keyboard from the center of the piano.

Escort the younger students to the left side of the piano (or guide the hands of the older students to the lowest notes) and ask them to find and play all the groups of two black keys going up. Please note that by using the term "going up" when there is no other way for the student to proceed, the concept of up and down will be reinforced. This is a common teaching technique that will be employed, the use of a previous concept in the context of a new one. It is the same approach used by teachers teaching vocabulary in school. Once a new word is introduced, it is immediately used in the context of a sentence. Context supports meaning.

Students can play each group of two black keys any way they like. They can use one hand and play both notes at the same time, or they can play each key in succession, or they can use two hands and mix up the playing style. It does not really matter. The focus of the drill is to help them locate each group of two black keys expeditiously.

Once students have successfully played each group of two black keys, have them do the same for each group of three black keys. Recognizing and playing each black key group are important rungs on our ladder. Therefore, students must demonstrate that they have truly grasped this concept before they can move on. Of course, complete mastery will in all probability come only after several weeks of drills.

When introducing the notes, keep in mind that "C" will be related to the group of two black keys and "F" will be related to the group of three black keys. Consequently, the introduction of the notes will actually reinforce the comprehension of the black key groupings.

The first note to be introduced is, of course, "C." So there is no confusion as to how the Discovery Learning technique works, let it be said that no matter what a teacher does, or what questions are asked, there is absolutely no way students can discover for themselves which note "C" is. Hence, a starting point will have to be given by telling students that C is the first white key before the group of two black keys. Once equipped with that information, students can be asked to find all the Cs on the piano. And, as a reward for finding all the Cs, students get to write C on all the Cs in their keyboard drawing. (If they have not yet learned how to write the letters of the alphabet, you may have to help them. In fact, you may even have to teach them how to write the letters as you go along. Oftentimes, even the youngest students already know the ABC Song, so teaching them the alphabet is not as difficult as one may expect!)

After the student has found all the Cs on the piano and has written "C" on each of the C keys in the manuscript book, write the following statement under the drawing:

The note "C" comes before the group of 2 black keys.

By writing this and similar statements into the student's book, parents will be able to help their children recall the process for finding each note. Bear in mind, parents are often learning the material at the same time as their children. For that reason, whenever a new concept is introduced, teachers must be sure to write it down somewhere in the music manuscript book or assignment book.

Now teachers can help students discover the note "D." It can be asked, "What letter comes after C in the alphabet?" The fact that the introduction of the notes has begun in the middle of the musical alphabet may cause some students to have temporary difficulty remembering which letter comes after C. If this occurs, sing the ABC Song with them and stop just before you get to D.

Once the student has figured out what letter comes after C, ask the question, "If C comes just before the group of two black keys, (it is okay to point to the note as you ask the question) then what note do you think 'D' is?" With a little help most students will be able to discover the "D" key.

Rather than relate the "D" key to the middle of the two black keys, students should be informed that the process for finding D is to first find C and then to play the note one key higher. In fact, the notes A, B, and E will also be found by first finding C. This way, students will be taught one basic process for figuring out a total of five notes.

Have them find all the Ds on the piano. Once that is done they can label the D keys in the manuscript book. Now write under the "C" note statement:

To find "D," first find "C," then go up one white key.

Use the same procedure to help students discover the note "E." Once all the Es have been played and the diagram has been labeled write:

To find "E," first find "C," then go up two white keys.

If students are young, the note "E" is a good place to stop. If they seem to be grasping the concepts quickly, then try moving ahead to the other notes. Either way, students are now ready to learn the first "Mystery Tune."

Mystery Tunes

Mystery Tunes are songs that students are already familiar with. But, because they are played so slowly when first being learned, are not easily recognizable. It is the student's challenge to figure out the title of the song.

The first Mystery Tune will be "Mary Had a Little Lamb." Since music notation has not as yet been introduced, the letter names will have to be written on the staff. Although we will want to switch over to music notation as soon as possible, writing the letter names on the staff in this way will reinforce the learning of the keys on the piano as well as sensitize the student to the fact that notes go up and down on the staff as they go up and down on the keyboard.

Also, keep in mind that the note "G" has not yet been introduced either. So, a little musical license will have to be exercised by replacing the two Gs with Es (2nd measure of the 2nd line). Once the student has learned the G notes, the teacher can correct the melody.

Teachers must be sure that their students understand what a Mystery Tune is. They can say, "Because you have done so well discovering the notes C, D, and E, you are now ready to play your first 'Mystery Tune.' A 'Mystery Tune' is a song that you already know, but because it will take some practice before you are able to play it smoothly, you may not recognize the tune at first. Your assignment is to figure out the title of the song!"

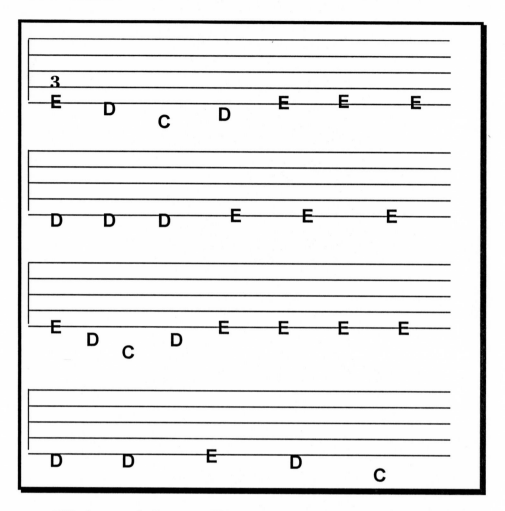

Kids love a challenge and Mystery Tunes provide them with just that!

Important point: Make sure your students play through the song before you move ahead to another part of the lesson. After reviewing the finger numbers, have students put their third finger on the first note E. Also, be sure the other fingers are placed over their respective notes. Next, using a pencil as a pointer, point to each note from above making sure that you do not obstruct the student's view. Have your students play and sing the notes at the same time.

The first time through will in all likelihood go quite slowly. Most children will swear that they have never heard the tune before. Assure them that they have. Use this same approach for all new Mystery Tunes. The only difference will be that once music notation has been introduced, songs will be written correctly, without the use of letters.

Let us review three very important points: First, always go over a piece with students before moving on to the next part of the assignment. Do not expect that they will be able to figure out the piece for themselves. Children (like adults) are afraid of the unknown and need to know that their assignment is achievable. Therefore, see that your students are able to play through each piece at the lesson. No need to review it several times; that is work to be done at home with the parent. One time is sufficient.

Second point: When you point to the notes, always point from above so that the student's view is unobstructed. The reason for pointing to the notes is that students' eyes have not as yet been trained to follow a succession of notes. If you do not point, your students will most likely lose their place on the page and get frustrated.

Last point: Always make sure that students sing the notes being played. No better time for ear training than the present! Remember, students need to develop the connection between mind and fingers; singing the notes as they are being played helps develop this valuable skill.

Introducing the Notes A, B, F and G

The same approach used for introducing the notes C, D and E will be used for the notes A, B, F and G. The only difference is that F will be related to the group of three black keys and G related to F.

When introducing the note "B," students can be asked, "What letter comes before "C" in the alphabet?" This is not an easy question to answer for most young students because they are actually being asked to recite the alphabet backwards. If they have difficulty determining that B comes before C, take a separate piece of paper and write down the alphabet, in order, A through G. Point to C and ask the question again. This time there should be no problem arriving at the correct response.

As with the previous notes, students must find all the Bs on the keyboard and then label the keyboard drawing in their book. Under the other note explanations write:

To find "B," first find "C," then go down one white key.

Repeat the above approach for "A." Then write in the book:

To find "A," first find "C," then go down two white keys.

Now we come to the notes "F" and "G." Students should relate "F" to the three black keys. The first and foremost reason for this is that F is simply too far away from C for C to be used as a starting point. The farther students have to count up or down from a note, the more likely they are to make mistakes. Besides, a good amount of time and energy has been expended making sure students can find the group of three black keys. Why not use that knowledge to provide a quick reference for finding "F?"

In this case, using only one process to figure out all the notes would take far too long and would also become quite arduous. So, a second process must be added. Direct students to look at their keyboard diagram with the notes A, B, C, D, and E labeled. They will notice that there are only two white keys left that have not been identified. Pointing to the "F" key ask, "What note comes after 'E' in the alphabet?" Once the blank white key has been determined to be the note "F," you can say, "We will locate 'F' on the piano a little differently. What group of black keys does the F note come before?"

Again, once all the Fs have been found on the piano and the diagram labeled, write in the book:

The note "F" comes before the group of three black keys.

Now, only the note "G" is left. Before repeating the discovery process for G, students should be prepared for the fact that the musical alphabet only goes from A to G. How is this done? By asking questions that will help them figure it out for themselves!

Have the student look at the keyboard diagram once again and ask, "How many notes are left that have not been identified?" Answer, "One." "What note comes after this blank note?" Answer, "The note 'A.'" "So, what does that tell us about the musical alphabet?" Answer, "There is only room for one more letter. That is why the musical alphabet only uses the first seven letters of the regular alphabet!"

The student is now ready to figure out what note comes after F and before A on the piano. If the student has come this far, figuring out the note "G" should be fairly easy.

Finally, students should find all the Gs on the keyboard and label the diagram. The last note explanation should read:

To find "G," first find "F," then go up one white key.

Once all the notes of the keyboard have been identified, teachers will want to go back to the first Mystery Tune and correct the Es that should have been Gs. You can simply cross out the Es and write G next to them, or you can erase the Es and replace them with the correct note. Whichever way you do it, make sure students know that the reason you wrote the song incorrectly is because the right note had not yet been introduced.

Reinforcing Note Recognition

Just because students have gone through the discovery process to identify the names of the keys on the piano does not mean recognition will be instantaneous. It is extremely important that students learn to recognize all the notes on the piano without any hesitation. To accomplish this, teachers will need to devise note recognition drills and games that will make the learning process fun.

The first drills are rather straightforward: Find all the notes on the piano in the following order: All the Cs, Ds, Es, Bs, As, Fs, and Gs—the same order the notes were first introduced. At future lessons, once students can demonstrate proficiency at this order, switch the assignment to: Find all the notes on the piano in this order: All the Cs, Gs, Ds, As, Es, Bs, and Fs (in fifth order).

While the above drills are being mastered students can play the following note recognition game at home with their parents.

The "First Person to 10 Points Wins" Game

The "First Person to 10 Points Wins" Game is a terrific way of involving the parent in the learning process. Here is how it is played: The student plays any note on the piano and holds it down. The parent has to guess what note it is. However, parents cannot look at the note until they have already given their best guess. Once they have guessed, they ask their child if they are correct. The child tells them, "Yes" or "No." If the parent guesses incorrectly, the student has a chance to steal the point by properly naming the note. However, if the parent guesses correctly, the parent gets the point. Of course, without being able to view the keyboard, parents have little chance of consistently guessing the notes correctly.

Once the parent has had his or her turn, it is the student's turn to guess. The parent now plays a note and holds it down until the student, who gets to look at the piano, guesses the note. If the student guesses correctly, he or she gets the point. The first person to reach ten points wins.

Just as with Mystery Tunes, children love a challenge. And, with the odds stacked in their favor, children should be able to win the "First Person to 10 Points Wins" game with no trouble. The slight competition that has been created will motivate the student to learn the notes. Bear in mind, competition has not been created to cause tension between student and parent; it has been created as a means of motivating students to learn their notes. It is the challenge that makes it fun!

Chapter Summary

Let us now review what we have learned in this chapter: If at all possible, parents should be made part of the learning process, observing at each lesson and functioning as the Teacher-at-Home.

Through the use of a Student Information Sheet, teachers should keep track of important information such as names, addresses, contact names and numbers, and dates of birth, etc. A List of Required Books and Music Aids must also be prepared so that parents can easily purchase the necessary items needed to facilitate the learning process at home and at the lesson.

At the first lesson, honesty between student and teacher must be stressed and teachers must make sure that parents understand that the ultimate goal of music instruction is to build a child's self-esteem by making piano a positive experience.

When introducing concepts and skills, teachers must show students how to break down each task into its component parts, helping them discover the answers one step at a time. This approach is often referred to as Discovery Learning and Step-by-Step teaching methodology.

Concepts and skills should be introduced at a pace that is right for each student. Each concept and skill should be reinforced with drills until they have been completely understood and internalized by the student. These drills may also come in the form of Mystery Tunes or games such as The First Person to 10 Points Wins game.

The goal of the first few lessons is to get students to start making music and to understand the basics. Theory and ear training should be taught concurrently with each assignment. Wherever possible, teachers should help students recall the process used to arrive at a correct response rather than having them memorize concept after concept.

Teachers should review each new piece with their students before moving ahead to another part of the lesson. By reviewing each piece, the fear of the unknown will be alleviated, and students will be made to feel that each assignment is truly achievable.

At the initial stages of lessons, teachers should point to the notes from above, making sure that the students' view is unobstructed. This will help train students' eyes to follow a succession of notes and make sure they do not lose their place on the page and experience unnecessary frustration.

Next chapter: The Introduction of Note Reading.

Chapter II-The Introduction of Note Reading

Years ago, when many of today's piano teachers first began their musical training, acronyms such as "Every-Good-Boy-Does-Fine" and "F-A-C-E" were taught as a way of facilitating the learning of the notes on the Grand Staff. Even today, the acronym method of teaching note reading is still quite prevalent and widespread. In fact, for many teachers, the thought of using another method is not even a consideration. But, is the teaching of acronyms really the best way to help students remember the notes of the staff?

The problem with acronyms is that students will often confuse one with another and thus misapply them. One would have to agree that Every-Good-Boy-Does-Fine and Good-Boys-Do-Fine-Always do sound rather similar. But, even if other less similar acronyms are taught, students must still learn to properly relate four acronyms to the lines and spaces of the Grand Staff in order to correctly identify the various notes. And, students quickly find out that just knowing the notes on the staff will not help them locate the corresponding keys on the piano.

There is a better way of teaching note reading to students; it is based on relating the notes of the Grand Staff to their respective clef signs. In conjunction with this approach, we will explore the use of not one, but two method books to facilitate the reading of music, as well as the establishment of six criteria to pass each piece. We will also look at the use of music flashcards to further drill note recognition.

Relating the Notes to Their Respective Clef Signs

In order for students to relate the notes of the Grand Staff to their respective clef signs, they must learn to refer to the Treble and Bass Clefs as the G Clef and F Clef. They must see that the clef signs are actually old style letters designed to point out their corresponding notes on the staff.

The G Clef tells us that the second line of whatever staff it is on is Treble G—the first G above middle C on the piano. Likewise, the F Clef sign tells us that the fourth line of whatever staff it is on is Bass F—the first F below middle C. These notes, Treble G and Bass F, are often referred to as "Landmark" notes.

To most students, the meaning of the word "landmark" is often obscure. So, teachers should help their students discover the meaning by asking a series of questions such as these: "Have you ever gone on a long car ride not knowing where you were going? And when you finally headed back home, have you ever noticed a building, or street sign, or something else that told you your home was near? Anything that helps us know where we are can be referred to as a 'landmark.' In music, we have landmarks, too; special signs called the G Clef and the F Clef that show us where the notes Treble G and Bass F are located."

When teaching students the clef signs and first landmark notes, we can borrow a similar approach to the one used for teaching the notes on the keyboard: Instead of handing out a picture of the Grand Staff with all the clefs and notes labeled, teachers can draw it step-by-step in the student's manuscript book, explaining the salient characteristics as they go along.

First, take two staffs and join them together with a bracket. Inform the students that the top set of lines is for the notes played by the right hand, also known as treble notes, and the bottom set of lines is for the notes played by the left hand, also known as bass notes (see illustration below).

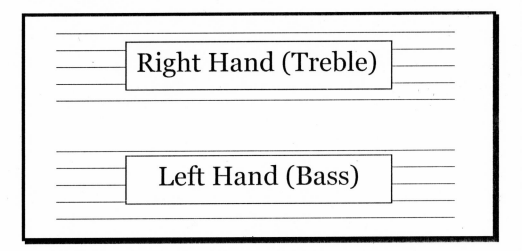

Next, on another set of staffs just below the previous illustration, place a big "G" on the top staff, and show your students how the G wraps around the second line of the Treble Clef and points out the note Treble G. As mentioned before, you will further need to explain that Treble G corresponds to the first G above middle C on the piano. Likewise, the big "F" placed on the bottom staff tells us that the note that goes on the line between the top and bottom part of the F is Bass F, the first F below middle C on the piano.

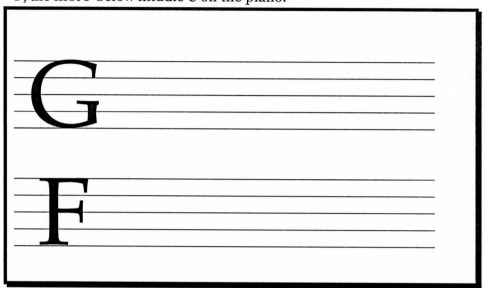

With the G and F already on their staffs, you can now draw a G Clef and F clef next to their respective letters and show your students how each clef is actually a fancy version of that letter. (The F Clef may be a bit difficult for students to relate to the letter F. One way of overcoming this is to draw connecting lines from the body of the clef to the two dots. Once the lines are drawn, the F clef will begin to look more like the letter F. Of course, it will have to be explained that over the centuries the connecting lines were dropped. Even so, the F clef is actually an old style F!)

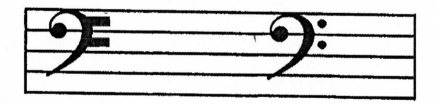

On a third illustration, a Grand Staff complete with Treble Clef and Bass Clef and the letters G and F deleted, place a note on each of the Treble G and Bass F lines.

It can now be clarified that the note Treble G will be the landmark note for the Right Hand and that this note is the first G above middle C on the piano. All the other notes in the Treble Clef can be figured out by simply knowing where Treble G is located.

Similarly, Bass F will be the landmark note for the Left Hand. Bass F is the note that goes on the fourth line (second line down from the top) of the Bass Clef, and is the same line that has the two dots of the "F" on the top and the bottom of it. By knowing where Bass F is, all the other notes of the Bass Clef can be figured out.

The concept of landmark notes will be reinforced as the notes Treble F down to middle C and Bass G up to middle C are introduced. Starting with Treble F, students can be asked the question, "If Treble G goes on the second line of the G Clef, what note do you think will go on the space just below it?" Answer, "F." (It is okay to point as you ask the various questions.) "And where is Treble F on the piano?" Students should play the correct note.

As the other notes are introduced, similar questions to the ones above can be asked. Asking questions will help students discover that each line and space on the staff represents an individual note on the piano; the higher we move up the staff, the higher we play on the piano; the lower we move down the staff, the lower we play on the piano. Make sure students play each note on the keyboard as it is identified on the staff; the connection between written note and played note must be continually reinforced at the early stages of lessons.

Learning to read music fluently with all its complex rhythms, ledger lines, and note combinations will of course take years of hard work and practice. So the next step on this demanding road is to select method books and flashcards that will ensure smooth and steady progress.

Selecting the Method Books

Digital technology brings new and exciting advancements to the piano-keyboard marketplace each year. As a result, learning to play piano continues to enjoy substantial increases in popularity. Music publishers, in an effort to cash in on this trend and increase their market share, are constantly developing piano methods that incorporate the latest technology into their learning systems. Therefore, it is imperative that we as teachers keep up with the latest innovations in our field.

There are several ways to do this. Probably the easiest way is to start by generating a list of music publishers via the Internet. Once a list has been developed, e-mails can be sent requesting sample copies of the publishers' various method books for your consideration. (It may be wise to include a little information about your credentials, number of students, etc. to give yourself some credibility.)

Another way of keeping current is to simply drive to your local music store and ask the counter person to show you all the different method books they have to offer. If you go this route, try not to go on a day or time when the store is likely to be very busy. It will be much easier to get the assistance you need when the counter person does not have several customers waiting. You may even decide to purchase a few of the method books so that you can review them in greater depth in the leisure of your own home.

Keep in mind that while technology will add to the fun of playing songs, it will never replace solid concept and skill exposition. In other words, there may be a place for piano methods that use midi files or other technology to accompany students, but the ability to incorporate technology should not be the determining factor in deciding which series you will use. Look for a method book that introduces concepts and skills in an orderly way, a way that makes sense to you. And you may even decide to use different method books by various publishers for different students depending on their age.

Most beginning piano method books can be put into one of three categories. The first category is where the two thumbs are placed over middle C. As the pieces proceed, new hand positions are introduced and the notes are expanded outward. The second category is where both hands start on Cs, one octave apart (the right hand starts on middle C and the left hand starts on the C below Bass F). The third category is where various hand positions are fixed around the landmark notes Treble G and Bass F and subsequent notes are introduced through intervals such as a 2nd, 3rd, 4th, 5th, etc.

The problem with method books that use the middle C or octave C approach is that because the hands are positioned over the same notes for so many beginning pieces, students have a tendency of identifying certain notes by the fingers played. In other words, instead of reading the music, they often substitute "hand position" for "note position." Students learn that their right hand thumb is C, their second finger is D, etc, etc. Of course this obstacle can be overcome through proper note drills. Nevertheless, why start out having to overcome the deficiencies of a particular method book.

One advantage that the C position method books have over those in the Landmark Note/Interval category is that their pieces have a tendency to sound more pleasing to the ear. It seems that composers of piano-method tunes find it far easier to come up with pieces that sound good and are liked by students when using one of the C hand positions. However, the use of Treble G and Bass F as starting positions have serious advantages over their counterparts in terms of their ability to get students to read music properly. So, what can be done to bridge this gap? Use a two-method book approach!

Select one method book from the Middle C or Octave C category so that students will play pieces that sound good to their ears; select another method book from the landmark note category so that students will not confuse note position with hand position.

A two-method-book approach works wonderfully. The other method book usually plugs whatever holes in the learning process are inherent in each book. Additionally, students get double the note and rhythm exercises. And, instead of flying through one book too quickly, the students' pace is slowed to the point that they are far more ready to handle the next skills being introduced.

Now, let us look more closely at methods that emphasize landmark notes and interval recognition. Why is interval recognition so important? Open any advanced level piano composition and play it on the piano. Are you reading the notes one note at a time? Of course not! To play a piece of music properly, one must read the distances and relationships between notes, not the individual notes. Therefore, whether we call an interval a second, or simply perceive that the notes are going up or down the scale, we are reading distances not notes. Interval or relationship reading is really speed-reading. No one plays a musical composition fluently by reading one note at a time.

In essence, method books that emphasize interval recognition are method books that teach speed-reading at the same time they teach regular note recognition. Therefore, the need for acronyms is completely circumvented. Students learn a simple process for recognizing any note on the staff: They start at the landmark note and then count up or down to the note in question. Soon, the counting process is replaced by the recognition of intervals and eventually note recognition becomes instantaneous. Whenever students stumble over a written note, they know that they can fall back on this simple process—a process that works equally well for both clefs.

The Criteria for Passing Pieces in the Method Books

One of the biggest mistakes piano teachers often make is that they allow their students to proceed from one piece to the next without established criteria for doing so. If students play each piece relatively well or if they have been working on one piece for too long, many teachers simply move the student ahead to the next piece without considering the long-term ramifications.

But, what are the lasting effects of moving ahead when the previous piece has not been mastered? First, students never develop a firm foundation to build on. Eventually the lack of skills catches up with them, which leads to disenfranchisement, thus causing them to quit. As they move ahead, they do so with a false sense of security, knowing in their heart that they have not fully mastered the skills or grasped the concepts at hand. Yet, they figure that if their teacher says it is okay to pass a piece then who are they to argue. Unfortunately, sooner or later these students compare themselves to their peers and conclude, in error, that they must not have half as much talent because they cannot play nearly as well.

Consequently, criteria must be established for passing pieces in the method books. Assignments must be broken down into sub-assignments, and students must be informed that they will not pass a piece until each aspect is done absolutely perfect (you can settle for 99.9% perfect, but do not tell that to your students!)

What are the criteria for passing each piece? Students must be able to 1) Point and Say each note, 2) Point and Say each note backwards, 3) Play and Sing each note, 4) Play and Count the rhythm out loud, 5) Play and Count at a minimum metronome speed of 100, and 6) Identify the intervals (for Interval Methods only).

When a beginning student has mastered all six criteria for a particular piece, both you and they will know that they are ready to proceed to the next piece in the book. Let us look a little more closely at the criteria and their importance.

Point and Say Each Note Forward and Backwards

If students were only to say or sing the notes as they played them, we would quickly find out that most students have the uncanny ability to see a note on the staff and play it on the piano without really knowing what note it is. We know this because when students are asked to name a note without playing it on the piano, they often have far more difficulty identifying the note than when allowed to play it also.

Remember, before students started to learn note reading on the staff, they were put through a number of note recognition drills on the keyboard. So, at the initial stages of music reading, note recognition on the piano is far stronger than note reading on the staff. How do students compensate for this? Let's say a note goes down one from the previous note on the staff. Students will glance down at the keyboard to see which note is one lower than the previous note played. This is not terrible; however, we do want them to recognize the written notes independently of the keyboard. Therefore, note recognition on the staff must be separated from note recognition on the piano. This is accomplished by making students point and say notes without playing them.

The requirement of Pointing and Saying Notes backwards is just another way of drilling and reinforcing note recognition on the staff. By "backwards" we mean starting at the end of the piece and working their way back to the beginning. I say this only because I once had a student who thought backwards meant facing his back to the keyboard and then somehow pointing to the notes on the page like he did for the regular Play and Say Notes drill.

Play and Sing Notes

Now that the evils of playing the notes as they are identified have been expounded, that is exactly what will be required next. Just to clarify, it was never stated that students should not play the notes as they name them. It was only said that they must be able to name the notes independently of playing them. So, why do we want them to also be able to sing the notes as they are being played? For three reasons: First, even after embarking on music notation, students still need to reinforce the recognition of notes on the piano for many months, until the keys become internalized. Playing the notes, as they are named, helps with that reinforcement.

The second reason for playing the notes as they are being named is that students must understand that the note they see on the staff corresponds to only one particular note on the piano. Playing the note as it is identified on the staff reinforces that concept.

The third and probably most important reason for singing the note names as they are played is that teachers should be teaching ear-training whenever possible. Making students sing the note as it is played is an effective way to train their ears without adding unnecessary drills to the practice sessions.

As with the next two criteria, Play and Count, and Play and Count with Metronome, students should not be allowed to look at their hands when playing and singing the notes; their gaze must be firmly planted on the written page. Teachers must help students get into the habit of putting the correct fingers over the proper notes before they start playing a piece. Then, once the hands are in position, students must keep on looking up. If students do glance down at their hands, they should be gently exhorted to continue looking only at the music. The same goes for the practice session; parents must make sure that their child does not get into bad habits during the week. In this respect, learning to play piano is like learning to type. If one constantly looks down at the letter keys, one will never learn to type quickly. Similarly, students who believe that they cannot play from the written page without looking down at the piano will be severely hindered in their efforts to learn to read music properly.

Play and Count

The fourth criterion for passing a piece is to play and count the rhythm out loud. Do not settle for students counting in their heads. If they cannot count it out loud, they do not understand the rhythm.

And, if you cannot hear them count, you cannot correct any mistakes that occur.

Rhythms are difficult. Do not be lulled into believing your students understand a particular rhythm if you cannot hear them count it.

Important note: It is all right to count along with students when you are first reviewing the piece at the lesson, or if they run into a particularly difficult passage. But, be forewarned, students will often stop their counting as you count with them. If you do help with the counting, drop out every few beats to make sure they continue counting also.

Play and Count with the Metronome

Here is a criterion that is sure to be controversial. Many piano teachers absolutely hate using a metronome in conjunction with any musical composition. They feel that metronomes make a student's playing sound mechanical and unmusical.

I can sympathize with this position. However, I believe that the benefits far outweigh the negatives. If a metronome is used correctly, it will help students learn to feel the beat and keep a steady tempo. Pianists who have not been brought up with metronomes are notorious for speeding up and slowing down.

Additionally, when used as a practice tool, the metronome can be started at a slow enough speed that students are forced to begin practicing at a manageable tempo. As the speed increases, students will know that progress is being made. Hence, the metronome acts as a means of quantizing students' progress.

For example, suppose one day a student is able to play a piece perfectly at speed 80, the next day a speed of 88 is reached. The student then knows that he or she is nearing the passing speed of 100. Sensing the achievement of the goal, the student decides to press on and practice a little harder, reaching speed 100. Without a metronome, students would have no way of knowing where they are in connection with their weeklong goal.

Once students have mastered a piece at a minimum metronome speed of 100, let them play the piece from that point on without the metronome, concentrating on all the dynamics. So, if used properly, a student's musicality should not be affected by the use of a metronome as a practice tool.

Just a few further tips on using a metronome effectively: Before requiring younger students to play pieces with the metronome, preliminary drills may have to be introduced to get them to feel the beat. These drills could involve clapping hands or playing single notes on beat at various speeds. If students have difficulty clapping on beat, clap along with them or, better yet, gently grab their hands and help them clap. Once students are ready to play pieces with the metronome, get them into the habit of counting one measure out loud, on beat before beginning, saying, "One, two, ready, go." If they are off beat before they start playing, their concentration will be diverted from reading the written music and frustration will surely ensue. So, the "One, two, ready, go" must be on beat before a student is allowed to continue.

One of the biggest mistakes students frequently make is that they start practicing at speeds that are too fast. Although they can play some sections of the piece at a relatively quick tempo, other parts must be slowed down. Therefore, a metronome speed of 60 is usually a good place to start; and even then, only after the piece can be played correctly without the metronome.

Once the piece can be played perfectly at the slower speeds, students can move the metronome up a few beats-per-minute at a time. Once they reach a point where they cannot go any faster, they can log that speed into their practice chart and start from that point at the next practice session. Even if only a few metronome clicks are achieved each day, students will know they are proceeding toward their goal. Once a speed of 100 is reached, with counting out loud, both student and teacher can feel confident that they are ready to move on to the next piece in the book.

Metronomes have one great attribute: they do not stop unless we stop them. So areas of a piece that have hesitation points can be quickly and easily identified. These areas would not be as easily recognized if a student's tempo had no frame of reference.

Point and Say the Intervals

The final criterion for passing a piece is to Point and Say the Intervals. We have dealt with it last as this criterion should only be used for method books that incorporate interval recognition into their methodology. When an interval is introduced in the interval-approach book, students can also identify that interval as it occurs in the pieces of the other method book. But, if students were to point and say all the intervals in pieces that contain 3rds, and 5ths, etc, when they have only learned 2nds, etc., chaos would result. So, interval identification is better kept to method books that introduce them in an orderly manner.

Though we have dealt with this criterion as the sixth and final criterion for passing pieces, when using an interval-oriented method book this criterion should be reviewed first at the lesson. Why? Students should tackle the easiest criteria first, and then move on to the more difficult ones. Pointing and saying the intervals is a far easier criterion than playing and counting at speed 100. Putting it afterwards would make it seem like an afterthought rather than part of a logical progression.

Music Flashcards

In addition to the establishment of criteria to pass pieces in the method books, further note recognition drills are necessary for students to learn to read music fluently. An effective way of drilling note recognition is through the use of music flashcards.

Many music stores stock several brands of flashcards. Will any brand do? Are some types better than others? What should teachers look for when selecting music flashcards for their students?

The first attribute to look for is that each note is positioned on the Grand Staff rather than an individual clef. When students are asked to identify a particular note they must be able to see its relationship to both clefs, not one. Most method books give students a Grand Staff to read from, even if a piece is situated entirely on one clef. Therefore, if at all possible, note recognition cards should follow the same format.

Students will make more mistakes identifying notes using flashcards that display only one clef. Without both staffs to view and give perspective, students are more likely to forget to look at the clef first before trying to identify the note. Transposition of clefs is a common mistake. Yet, even with both clefs present, many teachers will find it difficult to ascertain the source of this type of error when it occurs.

Some may say that forcing students to first look at the clef is a good thing. But, for the most part that is not how pianists read music. One clef may work fine for students studying flute, or for those students who only read Bass Clef, but not for piano. Piano music is written with both staffs, and flashcards should be viewed the same way.

Once the search has been narrowed down to flashcards that position each note on the Grand Staff, teachers must make sure that the cards are of sufficient size that students do not have to squint to read them. Most publishers take this into account when marketing their brand of flashcards, so this should not be a problem. But, be careful; make sure the cards are readable.

The next characteristic that sets one brand of flashcards apart from another is the way in which the answer is given on the back of each card. Some cards will simply say "D" or "E," etc. Preferably though, students will benefit from seeing a picture of the piano keyboard with the correct note highlighted as well as being given the letter name. Most sets of flashcards span a four-octave range (plus or minus two octaves from middle C). Therefore, there will be at least four different Cs, Ds, Es, etc to correctly locate on the keyboard. The placement of the note is every bit as important as the recognition of the note itself. Consequently, cards that give the answers in this form will be more effective than cards that do not use this format.

One brand of flashcards that possess the qualities set forth above is "Music Flashcards" by Jane Smisor Bastien, published by General Words and Music. If they or equivalent cards are not readily available at your local music store, ask the salesperson to special-order them for you. Do not settle for lesser quality flashcards just because they are the only ones available. Well-designed flashcards will make your job easier and the student's practicing more fun!

The Effective Use of Music Flashcards

Once the teacher has decided upon the type of flashcards to use, the next step is to determine how to effectively use these cards in conjunction with the introduction of notes in the method books.

As the landmark notes Treble G and Bass F are introduced, along with the two middle Cs (middle C as written in both clefs), corresponding note flashcards should be given to the student. Once the landmarks can be identified easily, the next group of cards to be introduced will be Treble D, E and F, and Bass G, A, and B, thus completing the sequence from middle C to each landmark note.

As new cards are added into the active group, they need to be distinguished from the other cards that have not as yet been assigned. Therefore, I suggest that a mark be made in either the upper right-hand or left-hand corner for all cards that are to be drilled. This way, should these cards get mixed in with the others, they could be easily retrieved. In addition, a rubber band could be put around the active cards and another around the inactive group.

Although we would expect to introduce new flashcards only as new notes are introduced in the method books, note recognition on the flashcards may actually proceed faster than in the method books. It is advisable not to hold students back in this area. When students can identify each note in the active group and play them correctly on the piano they are ready for two more cards—one note higher or lower in each clef. If any mistakes are made in either recognition or placement on the keyboard, then no new notes are to be given.

At the lesson, before the flashcards are reviewed, it is a good idea for teachers to shuffle the cards; teachers would not want to learn that their students somehow put the flashcards in an easy-to-recognize order. Additionally, should two consecutive notes be found one-after-another, after drilling, one of the cards should be put on the bottom of the pile. This way they will not continue to remain in consecutive order day after day.

Whenever students make a mistake in either the identification of a note or its placement on the keyboard, teachers should put that card in a "Do-Over" pile. Once all the cards have been reviewed, the cards that incurred mistakes should be reviewed once again and the teacher should discuss the source of the error with the student. Did the mistake occur because the student started counting from the wrong landmark note? Did the student count up when he or she should have counted down? Whatever the reason for the mistake, make sure students understand the correct process for identifying each note properly.

Also, any time a mistake occurs, the date of the error should be written on the back of the individual card. This way problem notes can be recognized more easily. The date should be written in a format that includes the year (it may take several years before the flashcards are finally mastered).

At home when students are practicing with their parents, all wrong notes should also be put in the do-over pile so that they can be reviewed a second time. However, there is no need to write the date on the back of the card during practice; the only times dates get written are when mistakes are made at the lesson. Otherwise, there would be so many dates on the back of each card that sooner or later there would be no room to see the answer.

Adding High G and Low F Landmarks

Once the notes that physically touch the staffs have been introduced, it is time to give students a new frame of reference for upper and lower ledger line notes. The new landmarks are High G and Low F.

37

If one gives thought to how octaves work on the staff, one will notice that if a note is found on a line then the octave above or below will occur on a space. This is an important concept for students to comprehend. Equipped with this knowledge teachers can help students discover that since Treble G is found on the second line of the Treble Clef, the octave above, High G, will sit on top of the Treble Clef (on a space).

Likewise, students must also discover that since Bass F sits on the 4th line of the Bass Clef, the octave below, Low F, will be found on the space just below the staff. Therefore, with Treble G and Bass F still acting as anchors, new landmarks of High G and Low F can be used for all notes that extend beyond the regular five lines of the staff. Once the High G and Low F landmarks are introduced, some students may find it easier to count up or down from these notes, especially when the note is more than halfway between the high and low landmarks on each staff.

Quantizing Progress—The Timing of Flashcards

Once all the note cards have been introduced, teachers need to find a way of determining whether or not progress is continuing. One way to do this is to keep a weekly record of the time it takes to name each note and find the corresponding key on the piano. A stopwatch with hundredths-of-a-second increments is preferable for this job.

Each week, in the back of the assignment book, record the time it takes the student to say and find each note on the piano. Make sure you record the date and number wrong as well. Students should be told not to rush unnecessarily; they should take as much time as they need to correctly name the note and find it on the piano. As the weeks go by, and recognition becomes faster and faster, the time it takes to complete the cards will naturally begin to lessen.

There is no need for students to get nervous. The only reason the cards are timed is so that teacher, student, and parent can see if progress is being made. Parents must not expect that times will be dramatically reduced each week. Rather, over the months a downward trend should develop.

Teachers can make the timing of flashcards fun by circling the time and date a New Record is achieved. A New Record would occur under two scenarios: If the student matches the same number wrong as achieved for their previous best, but beats the time, then a New Record occurs. If a student gets fewer cards wrong than he or she ever did before (that is, once the cards began being timed) then no matter what the time, a New Record is awarded.

Once students have named and located all notes correctly, then the only way to get a New Record is to beat the time. Remember, New Records are not based on a comparison to the previous week; they are based on a comparison to the student's previous best!

You will find that New Records are highly motivational. Students love to know that they have outdone themselves and achieved a personal best. With a record of the dates that these New Records occur, it will be easy for all involved to see progress being made.

Criteria for Passing Flashcards

How does a teacher know when it is time for a student to stop using flashcards? Answer: By setting a standard to "pass" flashcards. The standard I have always used and know for certain is achievable, is that students must be able to say each note and find it on the piano, without any mistakes, in less than one minute, three weeks in a row. Yes, I did say less than one minute, and I did say three weeks in a row.

What is the reason for "less than one minute" and "three weeks in a row?" First of all, note recognition must become virtually instantaneous. Finding thirty-eight or more flashcards in less than one minute assures teachers that students' note recognition skills are strong enough to do them some good.

The "three weeks in a row" criterion puts a little pressure on students and forces notes that are still weak to the surface. Many times students will get all the notes correct in the allotted time two weeks in a row only to find that the third week a mistake occurs. Granted, this can be a little frustrating. But, it will not be half as frustrating as when they have trouble identifying written notes later in life. Once students get to the point that they can identify all the notes correctly, in the allotted time three weeks in a row, they are ready to "pass" flashcards and go on "maintenance."

Maintenance

Maintenance is a one-year period where students need only to review their flashcards one time per week, unless errors occur or the time increases past the one-minute mark. Based on the student's flashcard performance at the lesson, the teacher adds an additional day of review for every note wrong and for every five seconds over one minute. For example, at the lesson the teacher times a student on maintenance at 59.62 seconds with one wrong. Since the time is still under one minute there is no need to add an extra day of review; but since the student did get one wrong, an extra day is added. So, for the upcoming week of practice, the student is required to do two days of flashcard review—one for the regular assignment and one for missing a note.

The maintenance period assures the teacher that students will not lose their note recognition skills. At the end of the year students get a final test. If all notes are correct, and the time is still under the one-minute mark, then maintenance is discontinued. If they fail the test, another year of maintenance is assigned.

All-in-all flashcards can play a critical role in training students to read music. Establishing criteria for passing flashcards is essential to that task.

One last tip on timing flashcards: The teacher is the one who should hold and change the cards as students are being timed. It would be highly unfair to expect students to switch cards as they are trying to find them on the piano. Teachers should also make sure that the parent could view the cards as they are being timed. Although parents will never be tested, they should still be able to see what is going on and possibly learn the notes along with their children.

Chapter Summary

Rather than using acronyms, all notes should be related to their respective clefs. The notes Treble G and Bass F will be referred to as Landmark Notes.

Not one, but two method books should be selected to guide students through the learning process—one from the C position category and one from the Landmark/Interval-approach category.

Six criteria should be strictly enforced for students to pass each piece. They are Point and Say the Intervals (for pieces in the Interval-approach method books only), Point and Say Notes Forward and Backwards, Play and Sing Notes, Play and Count, and Play and Count at a minimum metronome speed of 100.

Students should be taught to effectively use a metronome as a practice tool.

Music flashcards must be selected and integrated into the lesson-plan and practice sessions. Criteria must also be established for passing flashcards and entering a one-year maintenance phase.

Next Chapter: The Practice Chart and Student Progress Graph.

Chapter III-The Practice Chart & Student Progress Graph

The Practice Chart

Upon completion of each lesson, the assignments for the week need to be organized and communicated to students and parents. Some teachers choose to convey them orally; others opt to jot them down on the pages of the method books. Yet, for many teachers, the ideal method that encourages clarity and thereby minimizes misunderstandings is a centralized system known as the Practice Chart.

The way teachers utilize a Practice Chart depends upon their understanding of the difference between assigning an overall amount of practice time or a specific number of repetitions for each assignment. From Suzuki methodology[2] we find that the number of repetitions takes precedent over the amount of time practiced. At the beginning of the week, when the assignment is still new, it will take longer for students to complete the daily practice session than it will once they have completed several days of practicing. At the beginning of the practice week, a half-hour or an hour might be too short; at the end of the week it might be too long. That is why assigning a certain amount of practice time each day simply does not work. So, when the teacher is asked by the parent, "How much time should my child be practicing each day?" the answer should *not* be, "A half-hour" or "An hour," but rather, "As long as it takes to complete the number of repetitions assigned for each part of the lesson!"

As discussed in the previous chapter, each assignment in the method book must be broken down into six sub-assignments: Point and Say the Intervals, Point and Say the Notes, Point and Say Notes Backwards, Play and Sing the Notes, Play and Count, and Play and Count with Metronome. To assure that both student and parent understand how to practice properly, one step at a time, a number of daily repetitions must be assigned to each sub-assignment and written into the Practice Chart.

The concept of a Practice Chart is rather straightforward. In the student's assignment book, the teacher draws a blank Practice Chart (see Blank Practice Chart Template illustration). After reviewing the previous week's work, new assignments are added to the blank chart,

---

[2] Suzuki, Sinichi, "Nurtured By Love," University Press, 1969, p. 43.

one by one, and a horizontal line is drawn underneath each sub-assignment and across the page. Thus, a box is created for each task under each day of the week. During practice, students place a check or write in a metronome speed in the box that corresponds to the completed part of the assignment for that day. (See also illustration for Practice Chart with Sample Assignment.)

Blank Practice Chart Template

Week of _____

#	Assignment	S	M	T	W	Th	F	S

Practice Chart with Sample Assignment

Week of November 21-27

#	Assignment	S	M	T	W	Th	F	S
1)	**Book 1—Piece 1, "Up and Around"** Play & Count out loud—2X							
	Play & Count with metronome (Write in fastest speed done 2X perfectly)							
2)	**Book 1—Piece 2, "Riding a Bicycle"** Point & Say the Intervals							
	Point & Say Notes—1X							
	Point & Say Notes Backwards—1X							
	Play & Sing Notes-1X							
3)	**Book 2—Piece 1, "Going on a Vacation"** Play & Count out loud—2X							
	Play & Count and write in fastest speed done 2X perfectly							
4)	**Mystery Tune** Play and Sing Notes 2x (Figure out what song this is!)							
5)	**Flashcards** 1X Say Each Note, Find it on Piano, and check the back of the card to							

The Benefits of Utilizing a Practice Chart

Probably the most important advantage derived from utilizing a Practice Chart is that teachers have a means of analyzing students' practice habits. If only a few days are checked, the teacher knows not to expect a sterling performance at the lesson. If the lack of practice occurs week after week, it may be that the student is over-involved in other activities; or the parent may be the one over-committed and not able to find the time to review the assignment with his or her child. When a Practice Chart is used in conjunction with the Personal Scoring System and Student Progress Graph, (see the next section of this chapter) teachers will be able to show visually just how consistent practice, or lack of, affects a student's ability to progress.

If practicing is done only a few days per week and a student is still passing each assignment, it could mean that the workload is too light. Too light a workload translates into too slow a pace for that student. In such cases, teachers can add more work to the weekly assignment without fear of overburdening the student. However, the root cause for missing important practice days must still be addressed.

On the other hand, if a student is practicing almost every day, and yet has trouble passing each assignment, it could mean that either not enough repetitions were assigned for each sub-assignment or that the teacher is pushing the student too fast. It could also mean that the teacher has not taken a sufficient amount of time to explain and review the assignment properly at the lesson. **Analysis of a student's practice habits is the key to the correct pacing of that student. It is also the key to the teacher's ability to self-evaluate the effectiveness of his or her own teaching methods.**

What are the other benefits of using a Practice Chart? No longer can students say they practiced a greater number of days than they actually did; some students consider one or two days to be a full week of practice. By utilizing a Practice Chart, teachers get a true picture of the student's workweek, provided the chart is filled out accurately. Even so, the lack of practice is usually quite obvious at a lesson.

To avoid the possibility of misleading the teacher, students and parents should be told that assignments are to be checked off only upon completion, not before. Interruptions do occur that temporarily (or permanently) disrupt the practice session. By only checking off the part of the assignment that has already been completed, students are able to identify where they are in the practice session, thus making precise completion of the Practice Chart more likely. Additionally, if students do miss an entire day of practice then double the number of repetitions can be done the following day. In such instances, the missed day should be left blank and a double check put in the corresponding day's boxes.

Another feature of using a Practice Chart is that teachers can now assign the first three or four parts (of the six required to pass a piece in the method book) one week, and the next parts the following week. When students pass the easier criteria and are ready for the more difficult ones, the teacher can assign those to the current piece and move on to the next piece in the book, starting with the easier criteria for that week. In other words, a total assignment of six criteria can be divided between two pieces.

Depending on age, talent and commitment level from the parent, a teacher can custom-tailor a learning program for each student through use of a Practice Chart. But, as stated previously, the proper pacing of the student depends on the Practice Chart being filled out correctly. This is another reason why teachers must discuss with students the importance of honesty. Here, honesty comes in the form of an accurately filled out Practice Chart.

Another benefit of using a Practice Chart is that teachers will have an orderly way of reviewing the weekly assignments. If for any reason an assignment cannot be evaluated due to time constraints, it can be reassigned for the next week. To know where they left off, teachers can put a double line under the last assignment reviewed at the lesson. This way, at the next lesson, the beginning point will be easily identifiable. Teachers would not want to risk missing a part of the lesson two weeks in a row.

With so many concepts and skills to be developed, and so many pieces and drills to be assigned, it is understandable how a particular part of the lesson can inadvertently get dropped. By having one assignment book with all the Practice Charts in date order, if necessary, teachers can look back to prior weeks to see what has or has not been previously assigned. Of course, with the assignments written down in one central location, the chances of forgetting a part of the lesson will diminish greatly.

Although teachers will find that there are many more benefits associated with using a Practice Chart, the importance of clarity should not be underestimated. Teachers can write as much or as little as they deem necessary. If they write a great deal, all that happens is the corresponding box becomes larger and they may have to move to a two-page chart. Additionally, no longer will students be able to say that the teacher did not convey a key ingredient of a particular assignment, or that they did not understand the assignment correctly. Teachers can use as few or as many words as required for each student to fully understand exactly what it is they are to do.

The Student Progress Graph

The Student Progress Graph works in conjunction with a system of awarding scores for each assignment. We will refer to this system as the "Personal Scoring System." A student's Personal Score is not a grade, but rather a score based on the teacher's subjective determination of how well a student did in relation to his or her own unique gifts and abilities. The Personal Scoring System should be introduced within the first two months of lessons, once a weekly flow has been established and the teacher has developed a sense as to the amount of work the student is able to handle.

This is how it works: Students are told that if at the lesson all the parts of an assignment are done perfectly, they will receive a "Plus 3." If an assignment is done very well, but not quite perfect, they get a "Plus 2." If done only "Fair," they get a "Plus 1." No points for satisfactory. Students get a "Minus 1" if the assignment needs much more work, a "Minus 2" if done poorly, and a "Minus 3" if not done at all. As each assignment is reviewed, the teacher gives his or her evaluation by deciding upon a score and writing that number in the left-hand margin of the current week's Practice Chart (next to the corresponding assignment). At the end of the lesson, the scores are added up and divided by the total number of assignments to arrive at an average score. This average is the student's weekly Personal Score.

For example, suppose a student does all the sub-assignments related to the first book piece perfectly, and receives a "+3." Book piece two is very good, but not totally perfect, and thus receives a "+2." The other book pieces get a "+3" and a "+2" respectively, and flashcards are all named and located on the piano without error, thus giving them a "+3." Adding all the individual scores, we arrive at a total of 13 points. Dividing 13 by 5 (the total number of assignments), we come up with an average of 2.60. This number is the student's Personal Score for the week and gets plotted on the Student Progress Graph.

Looking at the Student Progress Graph (see illustration next page) we see that a score of 2.60 falls in the Excellent Range. Now student, parent, and teacher can say for sure that on this particular week the student truly did "Excellent."

With all "+3s" and "+2s," it is obvious that our hypothetical student did have a fine week. So, at this point some teachers are probably thinking, "I didn't need a Personal Score to tell me how well this student did."

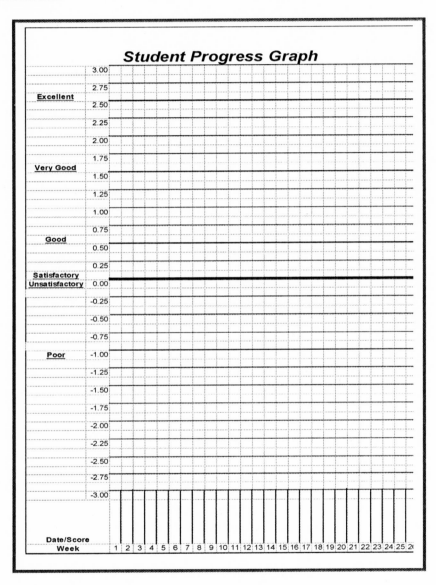

The real value of the Student Progress Chart is not that it tells all involved how students perform at a particular lesson, but how well students are performing over time. When lines are drawn to connect the scores week after week, trends become obvious that would not otherwise have been detected. For example, if the next week one of those "+3s" becomes a "+2," the total drops to 12 points, giving the student an average score of 2.40, pushing him or her down into the "Very Good" range. Should another "+3" turn into a "+2" the following week, the average score is reduced to a 2.20. At such time, the teacher, student, and parent will be able to see that a downward trend is starting to develop. With visible proof that the student's progress is going in the wrong direction, the problem can be corrected before it becomes too severe.

Most students will want to see their Personal Scores stay at least in the top of the "Very Good" range or, better yet, in the "Excellent" Range. Therefore, the Personal Scoring System when used in conjunction with the Student Progress Graph can be a highly motivational tool.

Students have a tendency to do the least amount of work to get by. When that occurs, the Student Progress Graph will bring it to light because students' Personal Scores are based on how well they are doing as compared to what they are *capable* of doing, as determined by the teacher. Thus, students are always competing against themselves!

Three final notes: First, one student's Personal Score should never be compared to that of another student, especially when siblings are involved. Each student's Personal Score is unique to that student and will vary as the teacher experiments with different workloads designed to optimize that student's pace.

Second, the Personal Scoring System can be employed for all ages, but is more effective for young students through the early adolescent years or until such time as students become self-motivated.

Third, the Student Progress Graph should be taped onto the front inside cover of the Assignment Book; this way it is always accessible. As subsequent Progress Graphs are utilized, they can be taped over the previous ones, thus keeping an ongoing record of the student's progress.

Bonus Points

Another great way of motivating students is through the awarding of Bonus Points. Bonus Points are points given to students for going over and above the call of duty. For example, suppose a student is working on a rather difficult piece in one of the method books. Normally the teacher would wait a week or two before assigning the hardest criterion such as Play and Count at speed 100.

The teacher can tell the student that during the current week counting with the metronome will not be expected. However, if the student is able to pass the first five criteria, he or she will be given a chance to get a Bonus Point by being able to Play and Count at a metronome speed of 80 or 100 (if 80, passing is still 100). But, it must be done perfectly within three tries!

Some students will rise to the challenge; others will not. The challenge to the teacher is to dangle the proverbial carrot just far enough away that students will strive to achieve the desired goal. If the Bonus Assignments are too difficult, students will not even try to complete them. If they are too easy, then Bonus Points will lose all meaning. So the idea is to stretch students through the use of bonus assignments that are reasonably achievable.

Bonus Points for bonus assignments can come in many forms. A Bonus Point could be awarded for memorizing an important piece. Or, one might be awarded for transposing a five-finger major pattern to another key or to all twelve keys. In fact, as students prove that they can handle easy bonus assignments, teachers can increase the difficulty for achieving the next Bonus Points.

Often, with Bonus Points added into the score, students literally go "off the graph." So, if motivation is the goal, Bonus Points are a means to the end. But, make sure the Bonus Assignments are feasible. As your students show you what they are capable of achieving, keep on stretching them. After a while, what once was considered to be a bonus assignment could become part of the regular lesson. Students will love the fact that they are able to accomplish far more than they ever expected. Teachers will find that as students achieve greater success at the piano, music will play an integral role in building their self-esteem. As that happens, students will begin to develop a deep and lasting love for their instrument.

Chapter Summary

A Practice Chart is an ideal way of communicating the weekly assignment to students. By dividing each assignment into its sub-assignments and allowing students to check off corresponding boxes on the chart, practice habits will become evident and misunderstandings will seemingly disappear.

Through the use of a Practice Chart, teachers will be able to analyze their students' practice habits and adjust their teaching accordingly. Consequently, teachers will be able to optimize each student's learning pace.

By incorporating the Personal Scoring System into the Student Progress Graph, teachers, students, and parents will be able to notice trends that would not otherwise have been easily identifiable.

By adding Bonus Points to the mix, teachers can motivate students to achieve far beyond what would normally have been expected. As students' accomplishments increase, their self-esteem will build, thus making piano a positive experience and an integral part of their lives.

Next Chapter: The Place of Popular Music in the Lesson Plan.

Chapter IV-The Place of Popular Music in the Lesson Plan

Is there a place for popular music in the lesson plan? The answer is a resounding "Yes," provided the lesson plan also includes method books, note recognition drills, scales, technique, and so forth. Through popular music teachers can emphasize learning to play by ear as well as the development of an improvisational style. Popular music can also be used as a tool to facilitate a basic understanding of harmonic theory. It should not, however, be used as the primary means of teaching note reading.

When note reading is taught through popular music, concepts and skills are introduced in a deleterious manner. Method books, on the other hand, introduce one new concept at a time, making them the far better choice to facilitate the learning of notes and rhythm. Yet, too often, traditional teachers put students through years of lessons thinking the goal is to make them into concert pianists. Consequently, the few students who actually learn to play proficiently become excellent sight-readers and interpreters of serious music but are completely unable to improvise a popular or jazz arrangement. This "serious-only" approach could be compared to a pre-med student learning nothing about doctoring other than the specific skills needed to become a heart-surgeon. Even our medical schools are learning the error of this sort of thinking.

Our goal should be to give students a musical "liberal arts" education during the beginning years and then to let them decide what area of specialization they would like to pursue. Agreed, this approach will not produce the next crop of award winning and world famous concert pianists; but it will produce a harvest of pianists that love music and are ready to handle virtually any challenge.

So, how do teachers go about incorporating popular music into the lesson plan? As soon as students can play a simple children's tune with singing the notes and/or words, they are ready to add in the chords. Yes, it is possible for students as young as three or four years of age to coordinate the use of both hands as they play the melody and chords together.

But, many will be thinking that a student of three or four years of age does not have the hand strength and coordination to play a major triad. This is quite true. However, the major-ness or minor-ness of a chord is not determined by playing all three notes of the triad, but rather by playing only the root and third. Therefore, when dealing with students who are young, two-note chords must be implemented.

Two-note chords are to be played with the left hand, using the middle and index fingers for strength and balance. Although it is not desirable to use two-note chords for any extended period of time, they are certainly useful in developing coordination, especially until such time as students develop the dexterity to play triads.

The benefits of using two-note chords far outweigh any potential negatives. Probably the most important benefit is that songs will sound much richer than the one-note-at-a-time music offered in the method books. Parents will be amazed that their children are actually able to play with both hands, like real pianists do. This sort of emotional boost will give students and parents the incentive to persevere when the first area of prolonged difficulty is reached.

Two-note chords can be taught by rote, leaving the theory to later when major triads are introduced. Chord symbols should be added to the music, above the notes, wherever they are to be played. It is also a good idea to circle the chords so that they can be distinguished easily from the notes of the melody (particularly if students are still reading from letters rather than musical notation).

So, popular music is initially added to the lesson plan through simple tunes and it continues with the introduction of triads and progressively more difficult songs. Eventually, students who prove to be diligent at practicing their entire assignment may be allowed to select the popular songs they would like to play. Of course, the pieces they select must lend themselves to being played on the piano.

Once the Children's Tune phase has been completed and before students are allowed to request their favorite songs, teachers may give their students another option, a list a three or four "pop classics" to choose from. If students are not familiar with the titles, teachers can play a shortened version of each piece. The list should be kept to pieces that fall within the students' skill range, with the more difficult pieces offered at a later time. During the holiday season popular tunes may take the form of holiday songs.

Once again, popular music should be *part* of the lesson, not *the* lesson. Teachers who capitulate to students in this area and teach them nothing but popular music do their students a great disservice. If students are truly to receive a "liberal arts" education in music, they must be trained in the classics as well; that is where the method books lead. And, it must be reiterated: Teachers should not use popular music as a primary means of teaching note and rhythmic reading. Note and rhythmic reading can only be properly taught through the orderly introduction of concepts and skills as presented in the method books. Once the method books have fulfilled their purpose, easy classics should replace them. (Some teachers may choose to introduce classical compositions while students are still using method books. If this is done, one method series should be dropped in favor of their classical counterparts.)

When playing popular music the goal is to make each song sound as close to the original recording as possible. As students advance they should be taught to incorporate pertinent bass and string lines, as well as rhythmic riffs, into the melody and harmony. Of course, this will take years of training to fully accomplish. But, as popular technique is developed, songs *will* begin to come to life.

Here, the ability of the teacher to demonstrate how the pieces should sound would be a great asset. However, for those teachers not versed in popular technique, there is no need to fear. All that needs to be done is to look carefully at a few popular arrangements and note how the arranger integrates the melody, chords, and bass lines, etc into the arrangement. A great deal can be learned from this sort of analysis.

There is no need to make students adhere to the same criteria for passing popular pieces as they do in the method books; all the fun would be taken away from playing the songs. The melodies should be played primarily by ear, using the written notes merely as a reference. The reason for this is that popular arrangements are seldom written the way the artist records them. So, let students use their ear as their guide. Rhythms should be counted out loud only in very limited instances—when the rhythmic patterns are integral to the piece and the degree of difficulty leaves you no other choice.

When making the transition to playing triads, students should initially play all chords with the left hand in root position as the right hand plays the melody. Stay away from inversions until such time as Slash/Chord notation is introduced in the more advanced popular arrangements. When chords are played in root position, the building of root, third, and fifth is continually reinforced, thereby allowing memorization to occur quickly. If inversions were to be introduced before memorization occurred, the memorization process would be derailed.

As part of developing popular technique, chord tones should eventually be distributed between the two hands. This is accomplished by slowly adding notes of the chord to the right hand underneath important notes of the melody. Once the left hand is freed from simply playing block chords, other fine points such as bass lines and countermelodies can be added. Through this method students learn to improvise popular arrangements that are always at their current level. That is why they should *not* be playing "easy" arrangements found in popular compilations. If they stick to an arranger's version of the song, they will be playing arrangements that are either slightly above or slightly below their skill level. And, they will never develop the ability to improvise an arrangement.

The "free-ness" of popular interpretation is in stark contrast to that of classical or serious music. In the classics, the pianist's job is to get in touch with the composer's genius by playing the music exactly as written on the page. Interpretation comes in the form of dynamic nuances, tempo changes, and the delicate balance of melody to harmony.

Just the opposite is true in popular interpretation. Students add dynamics, musical riffs, bass lines, countermelodies, etc, as their ability allows. If all this were to be written out in note form, the music would become far too difficult for most students to play at their current reading level. Reading ability almost always lags behind playing ability for the vast majority of students. Therefore, students must learn to improvise arrangements using the written music as a starting point, their knowledge of chords as a foundation, and their ear as a guide. As this is accomplished, improvised arrangements will bring an added degree of musical satisfaction to students' lives.

Finally, since many popular songs are harmonically quite simple, they are great vehicles for introducing beginning harmonic theory. Therefore, when a teacher senses that a student is ready, the I, IV, and V7 chords should be identified in each piece. Before too long, all the chords of the key can be introduced, as well as V of V chords, and modulations, etc.

Introducing Major Chords-The Four-Half-Step Three-Half-Step Rule

There are two usual ways of teaching major chords: They can be taught by rote, or they can be related to their respective major scales. The problem with teaching chords by rote is that students do not learn the theory behind what they are doing. Without the theory to back up the action, memorization is hindered, comprehension is shallow, and internalization takes far longer to achieve.

The problem with relating major chords to their respective scales is that the teacher cannot introduce all the chords until all the major scales have been taught. This could take years!

If we look at the first five notes of a major scale, we find that there are four half-steps from the root to the third, and three half-steps between the third and the fifth. Hence, if students are taught this four-half-step three-half-step rule, they will be able to figure out any major chord without having to know the entire scale.

The simplest explanation of a half-step is the best one for students to follow: A half-step is the distance from one note to another with *no* note in between. Teachers should make sure that the recognition of half-steps is sufficiently drilled before moving ahead. Students need to know that half-steps do not only occur between white and black keys; they could come between two white keys (i.e. B to C, and E to F).

Once students can demonstrate comprehension of half-steps, it is time to apply the four-half-step three-half-step rule to major chords. A two-hand approach seems to work best when counting out and playing major chords. Students should play the root of the chord with the pinky or fifth finger of their left hand. Then, using their right hand, they can count up four half-steps. (Make sure they understand that the counting of the half-steps begins with the next note, not the note played by their fifth finger.) Once they arrive at the third of the chord, the middle finger should be used to play that note. Finally, by counting up the remaining three half-steps, the fifth of the chord will be located. This note, of course, should be played with the thumb.

Now the major chord is complete; the root, third, and fifth have all been discovered and played with the proper fingers. Please note that the four-half-step three-half-step rule only works for major chords in root position. By learning major chords in this way, students will find it easier to relate them to their respective scales once those scales are introduced. The relationship between the different types of chords and their respective scales is one that will need to be extensively explored if students are to grow in their musical development.

Another reason why major chords should initially be taught only in root position is that as other types of chords are introduced they should be related to their corresponding major chord. For example, a minor chord should be seen as a major chord with a lowered third; an augmented chord should be understood as a major chord with a raised fifth, etc. Therefore, it is imperative that students learn to instantly recognize and play any major chord in root position.

One of the best books available on the market to drill not only major chords, but virtually every other chord and their related scales, is a book by Jerry Coker, et al, entitled "Patterns for Jazz," and published by Studio PR, a division of Warner Bros Publications. I highly recommend it. Be advised, this book deals with chords in their four-note versions, so it cannot be incorporated into the lesson plan until such time as a student's hand can traverse an octave.

Quantizing Progress-The Timing of Major Chord Orders

As soon as the four-half-step three-half-step rule is taught, students should be timed on Chord Order I as illustrated. This initial timing will give teachers and students a reference point so that progress (or lack of) can be ascertained week after week.

Chord Order I, as well as orders II, and III (once they are introduced) can be written on the back inside cover of the assignment book. Approximately three inches from the right end of the back inside cover, teachers should draw five vertical lines the length of the page, which will create a total of six columns. This is for keeping track of the dates and times of both chord orders and flashcards. See illustration.

Major Chord Practice Orders

		{Chords}			{Flashcards}	
	Date	I	II	III	Time	#Wrong

I.

C D♭ D E♭ E

F G♭ G A♭

A B♭ B C

II.

C F B♭ E♭ A♭

D♭ G♭ B E A

D G C

III.

C E♭ G♭ A

F A♭ B D

B♭ D♭ E G

Initially, only Chord Order I should be written onto the page; once the one-minute mark has been surpassed, the next chord order can be introduced. Also, when first playing a chord order, students should be timed using their left hand alone. Once they are able to play the chords in less than twenty seconds, they are ready to switch to playing them simultaneously with both hands. This will be a big jump in difficulty, so expect the times to jump way up again. Consequently, students may be temporarily working on one chord order with both hands while working on another with the left hand alone.

A chord order is officially passed when students can play it perfectly, using both hands, in less than ten seconds, three weeks in a row. At first, breaking the ten-second barrier will seem like an insurmountable feat to most students. Yet, with consistent practice it can be accomplished. The requiring of three weeks in a row puts necessary pressure on students. If an order breaks down on the third week and the time goes back up, then students are not yet ready to pass that order; it is that simple.

As with Music Flashcards, chord orders should be timed using a stopwatch that incorporates hundredths of a second. Just like in the Olympics, a hundredth of a second could determine a New Record. New Records should always be circled so that they are easily visible. Once a student switches over to playing an order with both hands simultaneously, the "hands together" best time becomes the one to beat in order to establish a New Record.

Once Chord Orders I-III have been assigned, teachers will need to draw another set of columns on a nearby page to record the dates and times for Chord Orders IV-VI.

So that students are not working on more than three chord orders at a time, the next group of chord orders should be introduced, one-at-a-time, as Chord Orders I-III are passed. In Chord Order IV, students learn to recognize chords by their "sharp" name. As you may have noticed, up until this point all chords have been called by their flat name. It would not have been wise to introduce the alternate name at an earlier time, as too much confusion would have occurred. By waiting until Chord Order IV to introduce the "sharp" name, the chords should be sufficiently memorized. Thus, the change in name should not affect students negatively. Teachers must help students understand that they are playing exactly the same chords they were before, just called by their *other* name.

In Chord Order IV, the roots move up by whole steps.

IV. C D E F# G# A# C

C# D# F G A B C#

Chord Order V moves the roots up a fifth:

V. C G D A E B

F# C# G# D# A# F C

Chord Order VI introduces minor chords. Through this order students learn that all they need to do is lower the middle note or third of a major chord to make it minor. (Notice the "Flat" name is used once again, so it will not be forgotten.)

VI. C Cm   D♭ D♭m D Dm   E♭ E♭m E Em

F Fm   G♭ G♭m G Gm   A♭ A♭m A Am

B♭ B♭m B Bm   C

Although this order is considerably longer than the others, students *will* be able to play it in less than ten seconds, too.

Once order number six has been passed, teachers have the option of repeating orders number one through five using minor chords or moving their students into the "Patterns for Jazz" book. Keep in mind that just because students can pass the chord orders in their three-note versions does not mean they have mastered major and minor chords. Completing the "Patterns" book is essential if students are to instantly recognize chords in symbol form via the written page. Instant recognition is the key to instantaneous use in an improvised popular or jazz arrangement.

Evaluating Children's Songs-The Difficulty Index

The last part of this chapter will deal with helping teachers evaluate the level of difficulty in children's songs through the establishment of a Difficulty Index. Method books take great pains to place songs in a logical order. Shouldn't we as teachers attempt to do the same with children's songs?

Here is how the Difficulty Index works: One point is given for each chord change that occurs in a piece, not each time a chord hits, but only when the chord changes. Two points are added for each hand position change that occurs. A hand position change is any time the right hand is required to move outside the first five notes of the scale or any movement from a new position.

Students often have difficulty when asked to switch their fingers to a new set of notes within a piece. For that reason, two points are added to the Difficulty Index each time this occurs.

Although not quite as difficult as hand position changes, the number of different chords that occur within a piece definitely affects the level of difficulty. Therefore, two points are added for each additional chord other than C and G.

The final difficulty category has to deal with the way the melody and harmony interact. Oftentimes in music temporary dissonances occur within a piece. The most common example is when a suspension occurs whereby the melody moves from a non-chordal tone up or down by step to a note in the chord. This tension and resolution found within a composition is directly related to the degree of sophistication and difficulty. Although trained ears are used to hearing non-chordal tones, most students think they are making a mistake when a dissonance first occurs. Therefore, we will award the Difficulty Index one additional point every time a temporary dissonance occurs as a chord is hit.

Now we will look at five children's songs and establish a Difficulty Index for each. The songs to be evaluated are, "Mary Had a Little Lamb," "When the Saints Come Marching In," "The Eency Weency Spider," "Jingle Bells," and "Twinkle Twinkle Little Star."

Looking closely at "Mary Had a Little Lamb," we find that there are a total of four chord changes, so that category gets four points. There are no hand position changes; the fingers stay over the same five notes for the entire piece. Therefore, the Hand Position Changes category gets a "0."

There are no other chords in this piece other than C and G, so we will put a "0" in the Additional Chords category. And the last category, the Number of Temporary Dissonances category, in this case also gets a "0."

So here is how the Difficulty Index for "Mary Had a Little Lamb" adds up:

Chord Changes: **4 Points**
Hand Position Changes: **0 Points**
Additional Chords: **0 Points**
<u>**Temporary Dissonances:**</u> <u>**0 Points**</u>
Difficulty Index: **4**

Next, we will do an analysis of, "When the Saints Come Marching In."

In the Chord Change Category, we find that there are a total of six chord changes. The right hand is confined to the first five notes of the scale, so there are no Hand Position Changes.

This tune incorporates the use of the IV chord, F. Therefore, we can put two points in the Additional Chords category. And finally, if one looks carefully, a temporary dissonance will be noticed at measure eleven, when the melody note G hits on the F chord. So, the Difficulty Index for "When the Saints Come Marching In" adds up in this way:

Chord Changes: **6 Points**
Hand Position Changes: **0 Points**
Additional Chords: **2 Points**
<u>**Temporary Dissonances:**</u> **1 Point**
Difficulty Index: **9**

At first glance, "When the Saints Come Marching In" may seem to be just as easy as "Mary Had a Little Lamb." But, according to the

Difficulty Index it is over twice as difficult! Now, we come to "The Eency Weency Spider" (a.k.a. "The Itsy Bitsy Spider.")

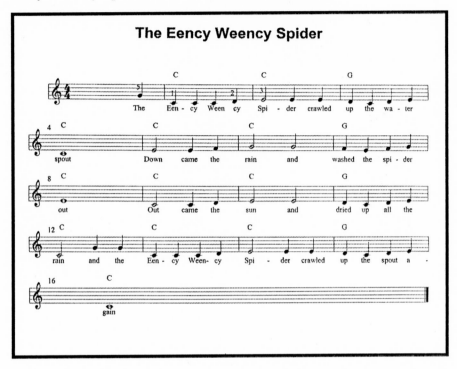

Once again, looking at the number of chord changes, we find that there are a total of eight. There are no hand position changes; the melody stays within the first five notes of the C scale; so the Hand Position Changes category gets a "0."

As far as the number of different chords is concerned, this song only uses the I and V chords. Thus, the Additional Chords category also gets a "0." And finally, there are no temporary dissonances for students to struggle with. So the Difficulty Index for "The Eency Weency Spider" adds up this way:

Chord Changes: **8 Points**
Hand Position Changes: **0 Points**
Additional Chords: **0 Points**
<u>**Temporary Dissonances:**</u> **0 Points**
Difficulty Index: **8**

Comparing this piece to "Mary Had a Little Lamb," we find that the only reason it is more difficult is because the song is longer and has more chord changes. But as far as the range of the melody, any additional chords, and the way the melody interacts with the chords, this song is equally as easy.

Comparing "The Eency Weency Spider" to "When the Saints Come Marching In," we find that although the piece is longer and has more chord changes, it has one less chord to deal with and the melody does not have any temporary dissonances, thus making it slightly easier overall. The fourth piece to be reviewed is "Jingle Bells."

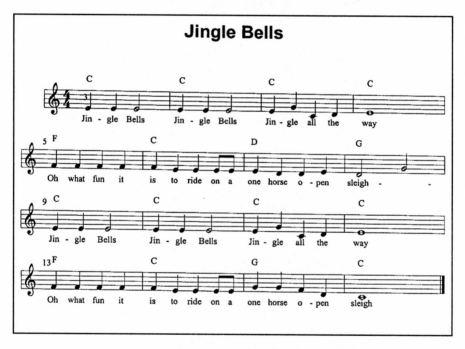

To play the song "Jingle Bells," students must change chord a total of nine times. The melody, though, is limited to the first five notes of the C scale, so there are no hand positions changes. However, it does incorporate a new chord, D, as well as the F chord, which also adds to its difficulty.

The interesting thing about "Jingle Bells," which makes it even more difficult than one would have expected, is that three temporary dissonances occur in the piece, at measures six, seven, and fourteen. Therefore, when taking into consideration all aspects of the piece, we find that "Jingle Bells" is four times harder than "Mary Had a Little

Lamb" and twice as difficult as "When the Saints Come Marching In" and "The Eency Weency Spider."

The Difficulty Index for "Jingle Bells:"

Chord Changes: **9 Points**
Hand Position Changes: **0 Points**
Additional Chords: **4 Points**
<u>**Temporary Dissonances: 3 Points**</u>
Difficulty Index: **16**

The final piece that will be reviewed at this time is the song, "Twinkle Twinkle Little Star."

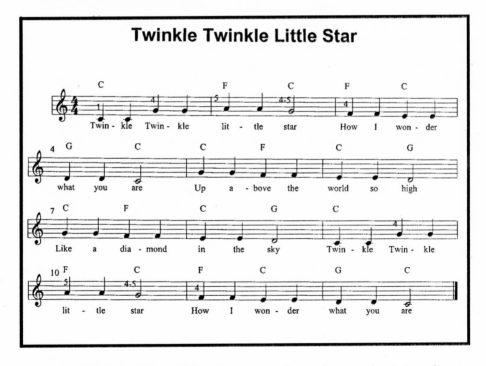

"Twinkle Twinkle Little Star" requires the student to change chords twenty times within the piece. For that reason alone, it is far more difficult than any piece reviewed so far. But, the real difficulty occurs when dealing with the hand position changes.

There are a number of different fingerings that could be used in this piece. An alternate set of fingerings would keep the fourth finger on the "G" in measures two and ten and adjust all the other fingers accordingly. If that fingering were to be used, it would create two additional hand position changes, thus adding greatly to its difficulty. Therefore, I have opted to switch the fourth finger to the fifth finger on the Gs in measures two and ten, thus keeping the hand in position for the rest of the notes of the phrase.

Even with switching the fourth to fifth fingers in measures two and ten, we must still consider the fact that the fourth finger must stretch up from C to G in both the first and ninth measures. These stretches will be counted as hand position changes.

The Difficulty Index for "Twinkle Twinkle Little Star:"

Chord Changes:	**20 Points**
Hand Position Changes:	**4 Points**
Additional Chords:	**2 Points**
Temporary Dissonances:	**0 Points**
Difficulty Index:	**26**

If the pieces reviewed in this chapter were the only ones to be introduced to students, then according to the Difficulty Index, teachers would want to first introduce, "Mary Had a Little Lamb," followed by "The Eency Weency Spider," "When the Saints Come Marching In," "Jingle Bells" and "Twinkle Twinkle Little Star" in that order.

Of course, you may have your favorite children's tune to teach to your students. That is fine; these songs were only used as an example. However, before you introduce any tune, make sure you have a good idea of exactly how easy or difficult it will be for your students to learn, and make sure you introduce it in logical sequence.

Chapter Summary

There *is* a place for popular music in the lesson plan. By allowing students to learn popular technique, teachers will be giving their students the equivalent of a liberal arts education in music during the beginning years of lessons.

For young students, chords should first be introduced in their two-note versions and incorporated into simple children's songs. Triads should be subsequently introduced using the four-half-step three-half-step rule.

Chord drills must be utilized so that students will learn to instantly recognize major chords in root position. All other types of chords should be seen as alterations to the major chord.

Children's songs can be put in logical order through simple analysis and use of the Difficulty Index.

When students outgrow children's songs, popular classics should be introduced. Eventually students may be allowed to choose the popular songs they would like to work on with their teacher.

When learning to play popular music, students should be taught to use their ear as much as possible to help them fill in the gaps between the written music and the recorded music. Students should learn to improvise an arrangement that is in keeping with their current level and which will, in most circumstances, far exceed that found in commercially available "easy" arrangements.

Next Chapter: Completing the Lesson Plan.

Chapter V-Completing the Lesson Plan

In this chapter we will look at the final two parts of the lesson plan for students in their first year of study. These concluding cogs of the wheel, so to speak, include the introduction of major scales and the requirement to memorize selected pieces.

Within a few months of starting lessons, students will be playing anywhere from two to four pieces in the method books, working on simple tunes with chords, practicing flashcards, and doing chord drills. This is no little amount of work. Yet, if these final two parts of the lesson plan are not made part of the overall teaching approach, there will be holes in the learning process and students will suffer for it in the long run.

The Introduction of Major Scales

Over the years, major scales have been such a staple of traditional teaching methods that most piano teachers introduce them to their students without having the slightest idea of their purpose or usefulness. Just as with note reading acronyms, teachers assume that because they were taught scales, they too should require them of their students.

Should major scales be included in the modern teacher's lesson plan? The answer is "No," if all that teachers are going to do is put their students through boring technical drills, which have no connection to the rest of the lesson. If, however, teachers are going to introduce scales so that they can be related to chords and harmonic theory, and use them as the basis of teaching transposition, then the learning of major scales can be a good thing—a very good thing.

Major scales should be introduced through five-finger major patterns once students are familiar with major triads. What is a five-finger major pattern? Simply put, it is any repetitive musical pattern that is limited to the first five notes of a major scale. The reason for this is twofold: First, without having to deal with the sixth, seven, and eighth notes of the scale, students do not have to concern themselves with fingering difficulties; they can concentrate on learning the notes. Secondly, since a major chord is the first, third, and fifth notes of a major scale, students will automatically know three of the first five notes, making the learning of five-finger patterns, in all keys, achievable, even at young ages.

Before embarking on five-finger major patterns, teachers can help familiarize students with the sound of a major scale through Discovery Learning techniques as they sing the universal "Do, Re, Me, Fa, Sol, La, Ti, Do" starting on C. Then students can position their left hand over a C major chord as teachers help them figure out the first five notes of the C major scale by ear. The teacher singing each note and the student matching the pitch on the piano accomplishes this.

Upon successful completion of the C major five-finger pattern, students should repeat the discovery process for the keys of G and D. Once the G and D patterns can be played correctly, it is time to discover the connection between chord and scale, as well as the half-step between scale degrees three and four. When students can see the chord in the scale and understand where the half-step is, they will be ready to conclude (with the teacher's help of course) that the same pattern occurs for every major scale. Students now have all the tools they need to play five-finger major patterns in all twelve keys.

To facilitate the learning of five-finger major patterns, I highly recommend the Dozen-A-Day Preparatory Book by Edna Mae Burnam, and published by Willis Music Co. This book is part of a series that introduces major patterns in the key of C and eventually leads to transposition into other keys. However, I have found that if students are prepared properly, transposition to all twelve keys can be initiated with the very first piece.

The playing of Dozen-A-Day songs in all twelve keys must be done one step-at-a-time. To begin, students should play the first piece "Walking" as written, in the key of C, at speeds 60 through 100. Once the key of C is mastered, the next white key of D can be assigned. Of course, teachers will want to walk their students through the first transposition. Students should identify the root, third, and fifth of the scale by setting their hand in position over the D chord. Then they should locate the half-step between F# and G. Once "Walking" can be played in the key of D, the process can be repeated for the key of E and assigned for the following week. Teachers might even consider offering bonus points to students who can also play the piece in the keys of F, G, A, and B by the next lesson.

As mentioned back in Chapter III, the awarding of bonus points often provides students with the motivation to work extra hard; in this case, the transposing of five-finger major patterns into multiple keys. In subsequent exercises, bonus points may only be awarded for figuring out all the black keys, with the white keys being the basic assignment. Even further down the line, all twelve keys might be assigned for each exercise and a single bonus point awarded if the next piece is completed in its entirety. Remember, bonus points are offered as a way of stretching students beyond what *they* think they are capable of doing; so at first, offer them liberally. Once students prove what they are capable of accomplishing, bonus points should be adjusted accordingly.

Not every exercise in the Dozen-A-Day Preparatory Book lends itself to being transposed to all twelve keys, so exercise some common sense. However, toward the middle of the book, the complete C major scale is introduced with proper fingering. Once that exercise has been transposed to the keys of G, D, A, and E, the four other scales that use the same fingering as C, it is time to include major scales as a separate category in the weekly assignment.

Just as with five-finger major patterns, major scales should be presented one scale at a time, only this time in sharp and flat order. The first five scales, C, G, D, A, and E, should be introduced, in their one-octave versions, first with the right hand, next with the left hand, and then hands together. Before jumping to two-octave scales, these scales must be mastered with the correct fingering, one note-per-beat, at 120.

The transition to two-octave scales, hands together, is often a tricky one; instead of having to deal with only one finger change in each hand, students now have to master three finger changes, in each hand, in each direction. Of course, the same finger changes that occur in the first two octaves also occur in the third and fourth octaves; so making those transitions will seem far easier when the time comes.

Using a C major scale, one way of facilitating the transition from one to two octaves is to have students place their hands over the second octave so they can see that the fingering is really the same as the first octave with two exceptions: In the right hand, the thumb replaces the fifth finger on the root of the second octave. In the left hand, since the thumb has already replaced the fifth finger when the second C is hit, the natural finger to play the next note, D, is the fourth. Another way of easing the transition from one to two octaves is for students to play the C major scale, two octaves in contrary motion, prior to attempting to play the hands together in similar motion. This is because in contrary motion the finger changes occur simultaneously in both hands.

When first learning to play two octave scales, students should start at the beginning of each scale and then stop on all notes where a finger change occurs. Each stopping point should be played three times-in-a-row perfectly at a metronome speed of 60. Once the first change is mastered, students can proceed directly to the next one, handling it similarly by again starting at the beginning and then stopping at that finger change. As far as the weekly assignment is concerned, teachers may want to assign a goal of completing hands together, two octaves ascending for the first week and descending for the following week. Of course, two octaves descending can always be given as a bonus point option.

The next scale, B major, should not be introduced until the prior scales can be played one and two octaves, with correct fingering, at a minimum speed of 80, at least three weeks in a row perfectly. Once the B scale is introduced, teachers should expect that the fingerings for the prior scales would start to incur mistakes. This is due to the effects of retroactive interference, which will be discussed in greater detail in the next chapter. But for now, suffice to say that the change of fingering in the left hand will wreak havoc on the pathways of the brain that control the fingerings for the prior scales. Therefore, as a rule, any new scale that incorporates a different fingering should only be introduced once the prior scales are absolutely secure. And, all prior scales must be constantly reviewed to make sure that they do not start to break down.

Once all the major scales are mastered one-octave one note-per-beat and two-octaves two notes-per-beat, teachers can then add three octaves three notes-per-beat and eventually four octaves four notes-per-beat to the mix. One mistake that teachers often make is that when they move to three and four octaves, they fail to require students to play the scales in the prior one and two octave versions. Surprisingly, when students reach the place where they are playing four octaves four notes-per-beat, they are often unable to play the one, two, and three-note versions correctly. Therefore, it is a good idea that each scale be practiced one-octave one note-per-beat up to four octaves four notes-per-beat consecutively (preferably without missing a beat) before reviewing the next scale. This may necessitate a little extra practice time, but it does hinder fingering errors from creeping back in. Once all versions are mastered, teachers can allow students to alternate the number of octaves they practice each week. Additionally, students should name the key signature and the number of sharps or flats in each scale before playing (that is until such time as teachers are certain memorization has occurred).

When students have mastered the playing of four-octaves four notes-per-beat for all twelve keys, the order of the scales must be mixed up to assure that they are not mindlessly playing exercises. Scales can be played in half-step order, by fifths, or by whole-steps, etc. If the order is not altered, there is the real possibility that students will only be able to play each scale correctly if done in a particular order.

One last note: Once major scales are introduced into the lesson plan and the notes and fingerings have been mastered, teachers should start emphasizing the different aspects of technique. Oneness of hands, evenness of motion, correct positioning of hands and fingers, etc, are all better addressed once students are able to take their focus off the notes and fingerings. This does not mean that technique cannot be discussed earlier; it only means that to stress technical issues at the early stages of learning would be overwhelming and counter-productive for most students.

Memorized Review Pieces

The final part of the lesson plan, at this early stage of a student's development, is the requirement to memorize selected pieces. What are the benefits of memorizing pieces?

First of all, when students play songs by memory, several different skills are reinforced. Probably the most important skill is the ability of the ear to direct the fingers. When songs are played by memory, there is no visual stimulus (the written page) in front of students to direct their way; thus the musical ear becomes the directing force. Therefore, reviewing memorized pieces without the aid of the written page is one of the most effective means of training a student's ear.

Are other skills employed when memorizing pieces? Yes, students learn to recognize melodic patterns and repeated phrases. They may also learn to see fingering sequences and harmonic patterns. Whether it is through the intellect or the musical ear, memorizing pieces develops the total musical person.

What are the other benefits of committing pieces to memory? If a student has a repertoire of memorized pieces, he or she can perform virtually anywhere there is a piano or keyboard. Additionally, when students are asked to perform for friends or relatives, they can play with the full assurance that they will receive accolades and praise. Therefore, requiring selected pieces be memorized is another way of building students' self-esteem. It is true that for many students performance can be stressful. However, when pieces are thoroughly memorized the stress level is greatly reduced. This same principle can be applied to many other aspects of life.

Let us not underestimate the effect that memorized pieces have on parents. Many parents live vicariously through their children.

When their children do well, they do well. Also, keep in mind that parents are committing a great deal of time and effort to practicing with their children, as well as incurring considerable cost. Therefore, when children are able perform for others, the parent's commitment is validated; all the hard work is worth the time, effort, and expense.

How many pieces should be memorized and how should the teacher keep track of them? There is no specific number of pieces that should be memorized; the number depends solely on the student. Some students may only be able to handle only one or two pieces at a time; other students will be able to handle considerably more.

When I first completed my Graduate work in Music Education, I decided to open a piano conservatory called The Malverne School of Music. One year I ran a contest for all my fellow teachers and their students: The student who memorized the most pieces by the end of the school year would receive a one-hundred dollar gift certificate to his or her favorite store. At the end of the contest I was happy to announce that the winning student memorized an unbelievable 108 pieces; I never expected anything close to that. In fact, the first runner-up also memorized an incredible 51 compositions, a tremendous feat as well.

I am sure that many teachers will argue the merits of running such a contest. However, the point is not whether the contest was a good or bad idea, it is that every student found out what they were capable of accomplishing, felt good about taking piano lessons, and felt good about themselves.

Now we come to the question of how should a teacher keep track of memorized pieces? In the back of the assignment book, a page or two in from the Major Chord Orders and Flashcard Time Log, teachers can draw a Memorized Piece Review List template (in landscape mode) across the page (see illustration).

When each piece is memorized it goes on this list. Then, each time a piece is reviewed at the lesson, under the date, the teacher writes in an evaluation. So that this evaluation does not get confused with the weekly Personal Score, the rating system for each memorized piece is far simpler. A "check," means the piece was played "Excellent"; a "?" says the piece was "Questionable," a "NW" tells us that the piece "Needs Work," and a "TF" means the piece has been "Totally Forgotten." (Once all review pieces are evaluated, the teacher can then give a Personal Score for the entire category.)

All "Questionable," "Needs Work" or "Totally Forgotten" pieces should be reassigned for the following week. "Checked" pieces might be reviewed by the teacher only once or twice per month, or even less if the list gets long. At the teacher's discretion, older and easier memorized pieces can come off the list as new ones are memorized. And, should the entire list become too time consuming, instead of reviewing every memorized piece each day, students may alternate pieces or groups of pieces.

Memorized Piece Review List

	Title	Date																							
1																									
2																									
3																									
4																									
5																									
6																									
7																									
8																									
9																									
10																									
11																									
12																									
13																									
14																									
15																									
16																									
17																									
18																									
19																									
20																									
21																									

"Check"=Exc, "?"=Questionable, "NW"=Needs Work, "TF"=Totally Forgotten

By using a Memorized Piece Review List, teachers will be able to assure that students develop a repertoire of tunes that they can play well. Eventually, as the degree of sophistication increases, previously memorized pieces can be replaced by more advanced compositions. Whether simple tunes or sophisticated pieces, teachers will have an orderly way of keeping track of each student's active repertoire.

Just a note: At the beginning stages of memorizing songs, teachers may have to help students along by working on one phrase at a time, alternating playing with and without music, etc. If one phrase seems to be too much to handle, students can try one measure at a time. Or, students can work on the right-hand alone, then the left. Remember, every task can be broken done into its component parts.

Chapter Summary

During the first year of study major scales and memorized pieces must be incorporated into the lesson plan.

Major scales should be introduced through five-finger major patterns once students are familiar with major triads. Students must learn to see the connection between scale and harmony.

Transposition to all twelve keys should be initiated through simple five-note exercises as soon as the chord-scale connection is understood. The half-step between scale degrees three and four should be identified.

Eventually, five-finger major patterns should be replaced by major scales. Major scales should be introduced one scale at a time, in sharp order, then in flat order, stopping temporarily at E, because of the left hand fingering change in the scale of B.

Technique should be emphasized and developed as students approach mastery of major scales.

Students must also develop a repertoire of pieces that can be played perfectly by memory.

Teachers can use a Memorized Piece Review List to keep track of all memorized pieces and to assure that each piece stays memorized and remains part of the students' repertoire.

Next chapter: Identifying and Overcoming the Effects of Proactive and Retroactive Interference.

Chapter VI-Identifying and Overcoming the Effects of Proactive and Retroactive Interference

In virtually every musical composition there are certain note combinations and phrases that are especially challenging and difficult to master. When teachers are familiar with a particular piece, they can almost predict in advance the areas where students will make mistakes. Yet, it is one thing to know where the problems occur; it is quite another thing to know how to correct them. And, it is even more difficult for teachers to know how to prepare students to overcome these challenges before they become unnecessarily frustrating.

Many areas of difficulty occur due to the effects of proactive and retroactive interference. Proactive interference refers to the negative effect that prior learning can have on one's ability to learn something new. Retroactive interference is just the opposite; it tells us that new learning may hinder the proper recall of previously learned material.

In the last chapter the introduction of major scales was reviewed. It was stated that before students should be allowed to learn the scale of five sharps, B, they must be absolutely sure of the fingerings for the scales of no sharps through four sharps. This is due to the fact that retroactive interference will cause the new B major fingering to impede the correct remembrance of the fingerings for the previously learned scales.

Specifically, how do proactive and retroactive interference affect learning? Using the B major scale as an example, the left hand starts on the fourth finger and crosses over onto the fifth note of the scale, F#, rather than the sixth note of the scale, as is the case with the scales of C through E. Additionally, when the second note of the scale is reached in the second octave, the third finger plays the C# rather than the fourth, thus causing confusion. As students practice the B scale, they condition their fingers to play certain notes. However, with the first five scales, students have already conditioned their fingers to act differently. Therefore, proactive interference, precipitated by prior conditioning, hinders students in their efforts to learn the new left-hand fingering for B. And once the B scale is mastered, retroactive interference causes the previously learned fingerings to break down.

In every scale, when the left hand thumb reaches the root of the second octave, the brain has a decision to make: What finger should it place on the next note? If the same finger is always used, the finger change can become automatic. However, once the B scale becomes

79

part of the equation, a new pathway has to be set up to direct a different finger to the second note of the scale. Therefore, the brain has new complexities to deal with as it learns that the second note of the scale only gets the fourth finger of the left-hand *if* the scale is C, G, D, A, or E; and it only gets the third finger if the scale is B.

We can think of brain pathways as if they are roads leading to particular destinations. Let us say that every time you drive to work and reach the corner of Main and Maple you make a left turn. Before too long the trip can be done blindfolded. If, however, on Thursdays it is your turn to pick up coffee for the office and a right turn is required instead, your brain has to be reprogrammed: Monday, Tuesday, Wednesday, and Friday, the route you follow must turn to the left; on Thursday it turns to the right. Therefore, because of the change of plan on Thursday, your brain has to set up two contingent pathways and know when to direct you to each.

Considering the complexities the human brain must handle, it is amazing that we as human beings can learn half the things we do. But, the brain is an incredible organ: We truly are fearfully and wonderfully made! Now, let us look at some other examples of proactive and retroactive interference:

One of the first notes students learn on the Grand Staff is, of course, middle C. Most students have no problem remembering that C is the first ledger line below the G clef. But, what happens when the first ledger line below the F Clef is introduced? All of a sudden the brain has to redefine its definition of middle C. Middle C is not just the first extension line below *a* staff; it is the first extension line below the G clef only. Hence, due to proactive interference, students must overcome thinking of low E as if it were a low C. And conversely, after the low E is learned they must not start thinking of middle C as if it were some sort of middle E (retroactive interference). When it comes to note recognition on the staff, you will find that proactive and retroactive interference are the source of virtually all clef transposition errors.

The effects of proactive and retroactive interference are positively ubiquitous. Take toddlers for example: When they initially learn the word for dog, their concept of dog extends to any four-legged animal. So, when they see a cat, they at first call it a "dog." If parents explain that dogs look one way and cats look another, toddlers must then learn to distinguish between the two and decide which is which. Now let us look at two other musical examples:

Looking at the third melodic phrase in J.S. Bach's "Minuet in G," you will notice that the melody moves from G in measure six to F# in measure seven. When a similar phrase repeats in measures thirteen through sixteen the G moves upward to A.

The first time it sees the phrase the brain learns that the G moves one way, and the next time it sees the phrase, it has to learn that the G moves another. Students will often confuse these two phrases and make mistakes. These errors occur because the prior learning that occurred in measures six to seven hinders the new learning in measures fifteen and sixteen. And, once the new learning has occurred in the latter measures, it will affect the proper recall of the corresponding phrase in the earlier measures.

If we look also at measures two and four, we find that the first time through phrases one and two, the left hand simply plays the note B. However, the second time the phrase occurs in measures nine through twelve, additional accompaniment notes are added. These are areas where interference is sure to occur.

Dino P. Ascari

Minuet in G

Now let us take a look at another example, a simplified version of Beethoven's Ode to Joy from his 9th Symphony, starting at measure nine:

On beats three, four, and one of the first two measures of the illustration, which corresponds to measures nine and ten of the piece, the melody moves from B to G, and then to A. In measures ten and eleven, the melodic sequence again repeats. The problem occurs when the sequence is altered in measures eleven and twelve; the A and the G are reversed. This is an area where students often encounter difficulty. Why? Because, by the time they reach measures eleven and twelve, students have already learned that the note G comes after the note B. Therefore, proactive interference hinders a student's ability to learn the melodic alteration.

How can teachers help their students overcome the effects of proactive and retroactive interference? Through Familiarization, Demonstration, and Effective Practice Techniques.

Familiarization

Before mistakes occur, teachers should familiarize themselves with some of the possible interference points. Just knowing what to look for is half the battle. When students do make mistakes, teachers should try to ascertain the reason why. Teachers should not simply assume that a mistake is a mistake; they must look closely to see if there are any interference points that students can be made aware of.

Demonstration

Teachers should demonstrate how the difficult areas should sound. They must also point out to students (and parents) how and where the melody changes. Teachers should further explain that due to the similarity of the phrases, mistakes are expected. Thus, students will not think that they are the only ones who will be having difficulty.

Teaching Students to Practice Effectively

Finally, once students are aware of the potential problems, they can practice each measure separately until the difficulty points are mastered. Should problems persist, teachers must train students in the use of effective practice techniques.

To overcome particularly challenging areas in a musical composition, students must follow these important steps: First, they must **isolate each problem area**. Next, they must start from the beginning of the phrase and **stop on each note where a mistake consistently occurs.** Last, they must play up to and including each stopping point **three-times-in-a-row perfectly** before moving ahead.

Isolate the Problem Area

One mistake students often make is that when they practice a piece, they start at the beginning and play it through to the end (or at least to the end of the assigned section). They think that if they play a piece enough times from start to finish the mistakes will magically disappear. Yes, it is more satisfying to play a piece from beginning to end. But, when students do not take the time to identify the problem spots and work on them specifically, the areas of difficulty drag on and on without ever getting resolved. Thus, frustration builds and playing piano becomes a chore. Therefore, it is imperative that teachers show students how to isolate problem areas and overcome whatever difficulties arise.

Stop on the Problem Note

Once a problem area has been identified, it must be overcome and mastered in the most expeditious way. Having students stop at each note where a mistake or hesitation consistently occurs and playing it three times-in-a-row perfectly accomplishes this. By stopping at the difficulty point, students place their entire focus on the problem at hand.

Three Times In-A-Row Perfectly

By requiring that the problem area be played three times-in-a-row perfectly, pressure is applied that will expose continued weakness. Once weaknesses are brought to light, they can be dealt with and corrected. Without pressure, there is no way to see if an area will break down. How often do students come into a lesson and play a piece that has been practiced, only to perform it poorly? What is the missing ingredient between practicing at home and performing for the teacher? Pressure! Pressure brings the weak areas to light.

If a plumber is called to identify a problem with a heating system, does he simply inspect the unit and give his report? Of course not! He blows air into the system and puts it under pressure to see if any leaks occur. If one blows up a balloon, does it burst after only a few blows? No, it is only when the pressure builds that the balloon bursts.

The same principle holds true for difficulty points in practice; they must be put under pressure to see if they will hold up. Students should count out loud along with a metronome as they work on the different sections. The reason for using a metronome is that it does not stop, but keeps on going, thereby revealing hesitation points. Without a metronome, students and teachers have no frame of reference to see if hesitations occur. Therefore a metronome must be an integral part of any practice session.

At any specific problem area, there may be multiple points where students may have to stop and practice three times-in-a-row perfectly. In fact, students may not even be able to handle a complete phrase or measure at a time; they may have to start from the prior note and eventually expand to the entire measure or phrase. Each problem area must be broken down into manageable pieces that can be mastered one step-at-a-time. Once the steps are identified and mastered, the area can be expanded little by little until the phrase can be played in its entirety.

Because of the effects of proactive and retroactive interference, the learning of similar but different phrases in a piece will cause each other to break down, even after the three times-in-a-row principle has been put into effect. When this happens, the affected area will have to be relearned using the same technique. Therefore, teachers should warn students in advance that even though they master a phrase once, they may still have to relearn it a second, or possibly a third time. The good news is that each time a problem area is revisited it usually takes half the time or less to relearn than it did previously.

This sort of practicing can be painstaking work. However, it will overcome any challenging area. But most importantly, students learn the value of efficient practice. Therefore, it is of utmost importance that teachers help students develop a mechanism for overcoming areas of difficulty.

When first beginning a piece, it is a good idea for students to play it through once with the hands together in the teacher's presence, so that the teacher can ascertain the status of the student's sight-reading ability. As long as students can read through the piece acceptably well for their current level, then no remedial steps need to be taken. If not, teachers may need to add sight-reading exercises into the lesson mix.

Once the initial run-through has been completed, teachers can make a judgment call as to what the first assignment should be. The vast majority of students will not be ready to practice most pieces hands together. In such cases, teachers should assign a manageable portion of the piece, hands separately, with counting out loud. Teachers can then add a note in the assignment book, "If possible, add in metronome with counting at speed 60," or "Goal for the week—Hands Together with counting at 60." This way, students will know to initially work on the hands separately and then try their best to get it hands together by the end of the practice week.

Also, before students begin practicing any difficult piece with both hands, they should be able to master the right hand and left hand alone, with counting out loud, at speeds 60 to 120. At 120, students can be allowed to count to themselves, as long as they play the rhythms correctly. (This is because the quicker the tempo the more difficult it is to count it out loud.) The general rule-of-thumb for switching from practicing hands separately to hands together is that students must be able to play hands separately at least twice the speed they will begin working at hands together. In other words, students should not try practicing with both hands at 60 until they can master the hands separately at 120.

It would seem from this rule-of-thumb that playing a piece hands together is twice as difficult as playing it hands separately. But, the switching from hands separately to hands together is far more than two times as difficult. If one had to venture a guess, playing a piece hands together is anywhere from three to ten times more difficult than simply playing it hands separately. Using that line of reasoning, students would then have to play pieces hands separately at speeds anywhere from 180 to 1200 before attempting to play them hands together at 60. Obviously, that would never happen; so the 120-to-60 rule is a good one to adhere to.

Chapter Summary

Proactive and Retroactive Interference are the source of many learning difficulties and therefore cause much musical frustration.

Teachers should look for areas in pieces where proactive and retroactive interference are sure to occur. After familiarizing themselves with the potential problem spots, they can make students aware of the difficult areas and demonstrate how the piece is properly played.

For especially challenging sections, teachers must show students how to overcome seemingly insurmountable problems through efficient practice techniques.

Efficient practicing involves isolating the problem area, breaking it down into manageable bits, and stopping on each problem note until it can be played three times-in-a-row perfectly with counting and metronome.

Next Chapter: Additional Motivational Tools

Chapter VII-Additional Motivational Tools

In this chapter we will look at three additional motivational tools: the warmth and caring of the teacher, the use of praise, and the running of recitals as a means of encouraging healthy competition. But, before these tools can be discussed, we must take a quick look at the value of extrinsic versus intrinsic motivation.

Extrinsic motivation refers to those influences that motivate a person from the outside. Intrinsic motivation refers to the motivation that comes from within.

Extrinsic motivation can take the form of awards, certificates, gifts, sweets, or other incentives. With little effort, teachers could find a multitude of items to choose from in catalogs or novelty stores that could easily spur on students temporarily. But is there any real value to the use of extrinsic motivation?

When students receive awards or certificates for jobs well done, the thrill only lasts a short period of time. If teachers offer students candies or other goodies when assignments are played correctly, they may achieve short-term results, but the problem of long-term motivation will remain ignored. Parents often make the mistake of offering their children money or special gifts in exchange for passing a test or for getting an "A" on their report card. They, too, soon find out that the use of extrinsic motivation simply does not work for the long-term.

To develop intrinsic motivation, teachers must find ways of getting students to *want* to achieve, from within. Intrinsic motivation is produced as students learn to persevere through the years of study to get to the point where playing piano, even at advanced levels, is more fun than work. Of course, learning should be fun from the start. But, if we were to be honest with ourselves, we would have to admit that it is much nicer to have already mastered the material than to learn it all over again.

In previous chapters we have looked at the correct pacing of students, the use of Progress Graphs and Bonus Points, the timing of Flashcards and Chord Orders, the use of two-note chords at the early stages of lessons, etc. Yet, to this point, we have not formally identified the number one motivational tool available to all teachers. What do these tools and techniques have in common? They all help students build a healthy self-esteem through successful achievement at the piano. This sort of success is not to be confused with the success that comes with fame or financial wealth. This is the success derived by overcoming obstacles one step at a time. It helps students build self-confidence and know that anything they set their mind to can be accomplished. Helping students feel good about themselves is the number one motivational tool that teachers can employ. Of course, this is often easier said than done. But, when students feel successful at the piano, intrinsic motivation develops accordingly.

The Warmth and Caring of the Teacher as a Motivational Tool

It may seem odd to call the use of warmth and caring a motivational tool, but the fact is that human beings respond to love and tenderness. There is nothing like a genuine smile to warm a student's heart. When a teacher exhibits an unadulterated attitude of caring, students will want to do their best. Therefore, do not underestimate how your own attitude will affect that of your students.

When a student likes his or her teacher, he or she will naturally strive to gain the teacher's approval. However, the teacher must demonstrate at all times that the student already has the teacher's approval as a person. There can be no question in the student's mind that he or she has value or worth in the teacher's eyes. Teachers can and should communicate their displeasure when students perform below their ability, but the student's innate worth should never be in question.

Teachers must also communicate to students that they are committed to them for the long run. There is nothing more devastating for students than having a teacher discontinue lessons once a sincere affection has been developed. Therefore, if you know that you will be unable to continue teaching in the near future, it is imperative that you inform your students as far in advance as possible. Make sure each one understands that your decision to stop teaching, even if only temporarily, has nothing to do with them, but is due to other factors. At the same time, it can be made clear that you want to make the most of your time together and expect to make great progress in the weeks or months ahead.

Additionally, if you as teacher have such a busy schedule that you will be forced to miss numerous lessons, you must discuss this in advance as well with both students and parents. Children often misinterpret teachers' continual absences as a sign that they do not really care about them and that commitment is not important. Should students feel this way, they will certainly not perform at optimal levels. Therefore, the relationship that the teacher has with the student, and the warmth and caring that is exhibited, will be a substantial influence on the student, either positive or negative.

The Use of Praise

Human beings love praise. In fact, we long for the approval of those we deem important to us. But, for some reason many parents are afraid of letting words of praise flow from their lips. Maybe, it is the way they were brought up; or maybe it is due to other factors, but for some mysterious reason, the sweet song of praise seems to be hidden from the hallways of many households.

Teachers cannot afford to make the same mistake. The proper use of praise will be one of the most significant factors in motivating students. But, do beware, there are dangers at each extreme; too much praise can be as counterproductive as too little praise.

Some teachers, all with the best of intentions, praise their students constantly for any and every possible reason. A student could play a simple quarter-note rhythm correctly when he or she has already tackled eighth-note rhythms, but may still hear words of praise lavished on him or her. Or, a student may have mastered a scale at speed 60 one week, be given the goal of reaching 80 the following week, only to come into the lesson playing it at speed 63. Although, this achievement is far below what the student is capable of, many teachers will still praise the student as if he or she had written a Bach cantata. Words such as, "That was wonderful," or "I am so proud of you, that was just great," are not appropriate if the accomplishment is below the student's capabilities.

When teachers praise students for achievements that are far below their abilities, it lulls them into the belief that sub-par performance is acceptable. Yes, encouragement and exhortation are appropriate, but praise certainly is not!

On the other hand, many teachers operate under the erroneous conclusion that if they praise their students at all, or under very limited circumstances, the incentive to work hard will be taken away and students will progress at a much slower rate. They believe the objective is to achieve some degree of proficiency or virtuosity, or to be the best, and have lost sight of developing the love for the instrument. When students truly learn to love their instrument and music in general, they will want to do their best. When praise is withheld, students will work hard, but for the wrong reasons; they will try to gain the approval of the teacher or parent. With regard to music, the result is students who can often play well but hate the instrument.

Some may say that the word "hate" is too strong a word. But, I can only respond by saying that I have seen it all too many times. Let me give you an example:

Back in high school, I had a friend who practiced five hours per day. In the tenth grade he was already performing Gershwin's "Rhapsody in Blue" at Carnegie Hall. This friend was one of the most talented individuals I had ever met. Then, many years later, at my ten-year class reunion we got a chance to chat. I was curious as to why I had not seen his name floating around the trade papers or on the lists of award recipients. He answered me with a sad but straight-forward response, "I quit piano and became a doctor." So flabber-gasted by his response, I followed-up with, "How could this be; you were one of the most talented pianists I had ever come across?" Again, the candid answer, "I just didn't like the piano; in fact I hated the instrument."

What a travesty! How could someone who was willing to practice so assiduously ever want to quit piano? Evidently, he was never taught to love the instrument and to play from his heart; his success was gained for all the wrong reasons: to win the approval of his parents and teacher. Or, possibly, so much pressure was placed on him to succeed according to the world's standards that any love he had for the instrument was lost and replaced by disgust.

I learned an important lesson from that conversation: teachers cannot use the withholding of praise as a means of motivating their students. Playing on a student's desire to gain approval either consciously or subconsciously is positively counterproductive.

So, what is the proper use of praise? Students should be praised liberally when the achievement is in relation to or beyond their expected capabilities. In other words, if a student meets or beats your expectations (based on your assessment of his or her unique talents) then use praise, and use it without reservation. If however, a student is performing below his or her abilities, then be encouraging, but do not use praise. Keep this saying in mind: Always be encouraging, but not always praising!

The Running of Recitals as a Motivational Tool

Recitals can be another highly motivational tool. Of course, if undue emphasis is placed on them the results could be negative rather than positive. We can think of any motivational tool as being analogous to toasting bread. If one puts a slice of bread in a toaster and then takes it out after only a few seconds, then no toasting has occurred. However, if that same piece of bread is left in for too long, it gets burned and charred and can only be thrown away. Motivational tools often work the same way. Use them too little and you might as well not use them at all; use them too much or inappropriately and the results are often negative.

What are the positives of running a recital? First of all, students have a goal to work for. Just knowing that one is going to have to perform in front of his or her peers (and their parents) can often have a highly motivating effect. This same holds true for other competitions or school-based adjudications such as New York's "NYSSMA" awards. With the running of recitals, students have a focal point to strive for. On a specific day, at a specific time, they will have to perform; so they better be ready. No longer can students adopt an attitude that when a piece gets done, it is done. The recital is the performance date; no extensions, no excuses; it is time to produce.

Unfortunately, teachers often realize that at a recital their students will either make them look good or bad and start to place undue emphasis and pressure on the recital piece. They make it clear in various ways that success among one's peers or success in the public's eye is the only thing that counts. When this happens, the excitement and anticipation of performing at a recital becomes corrupted and what could have been a positive experience for the student becomes a negative one.

Recitals must be kept pure. Teachers should exhort students to do their best, but the lesson plan must be kept intact. A recital piece is just another piece taken from the Memorized Piece Review List and brought to a slightly higher level so that it can be performed in public.

When selecting a recital piece, teachers should help students choose a piece that will be mastered at least one month prior to the recital. Picking a piece that is due to be perfected on the date of the recital is far too risky. Most pieces need to go through a process of breaking down and re-mastering, where mistakes start to occur once again, thereby necessitating the piece be relearned and re-perfected. If a piece has not gone through the re-mastering process, the chance of it breaking down under the pressure of a recital is quite high. However, playing it safe and choosing a piece that has been mastered months prior takes away the goal of working on a special piece. Recital pieces should be the students' best pieces, not their easiest pieces. Teachers should encourage their students to "go for the brass ring," to do their best, and to shine!

What are the other benefits of performing at a recital? At a recital, students (along with their parents) get to see themselves in perspective. In other words, they get to evaluate themselves not only in relationship to their peers, but to other students both older and younger. From the older and more advanced students, younger pianists get to see the value of diligent practice. Older students, on the other hand, get to see how quickly some of the younger students are progressing.

After performing at a recital, I have often seen older students motivated by peer competition suddenly adopt a renewed work ethic. I have also seen many of the younger students decide that they would like to be as good as one of the older students and step up their work habits as well. Yes, sometimes the "pumping-up" only lasts a short time. But, each time a student attends and performs at a recital, they get a fresh dose of reality. No one likes to come up short. For that reason, recitals foster healthy competition.

Another valuable reason for running a recital is that younger students get to hear first-hand some possible future repertoire pieces. For weeks after the running of a recital, I have often heard students ask the various names of the pieces played by the different participants and whether or not it is possible for them to play those pieces also.

One more benefit of running a recital is that students get to find out how they perform under pressure. That is another reason why the piece they play must be completely memorized at least one month prior to being performed. It is one thing to think you know how you will perform under pressure; it is another thing to actually do it. Therefore, teachers must adequately prepare students for performing at the recital and must make sure that any weak areas are addressed and cleaned up. Each time students handle pressure successfully it gets a little easier for them to handle it the next time.

Should a student perform poorly at the recital, an opportunity is created to discuss the reasons why and correct the deficiencies for the next time. I have often seen students who have performed below their abilities one year come back the next to give a wonderful performance. It seems that many times in life our failures teach us more than our successes.

If used as one of many motivational tools, recitals can be highly positive experiences, which will be carried into adulthood. They create anticipation of the good things to come and allow students to put themselves into perspective—a perspective that cannot be achieved anywhere else in music during the growing years.

Recital Preparation and Planning

When running a recital, there is a certain amount of preparation and planning that is required in order to assure that the experience will be a positive one for all involved.

First, a recital date will have to be selected. What usually works best is for teachers to run their recitals a few weeks before the end of a school year. When a recital is held too far in advance of the school year end it tends to be viewed as anticlimactic. If held after the school year is completed, many students and parents will have already planned their vacations and may be away. When recitals are held in the middle of the school year or during the winter recess, students may feel that they do not have adequate time to prepare, thus undue pressure is created; and mid-year vacations may once again present a problem. However, whatever date is selected, students must be given plenty of advance warning. As soon as all decisions have been made pertaining to the running of the recital, a simple flyer listing logistical information as well as directions to the recital hall should be handed out to students or sent home via e-mail or conventional mail.

Teachers must determine how many students will actually perform in the recital. Students should be exhorted to take part in the program, but under no circumstances should they be forced to perform. This is not to say that teachers should simply take "no" as an answer when confronted by those students who exhibit reluctance to making a recital commitment. There is nothing wrong with discussing all the positive benefits that will be gained from being part of the festivities. However, in cases where there is an irrational fear of being in front of people or where there is a legitimate reason that prevents a student from performing, teachers should insist that those students at least attend the recital and sit in the audience. Many times, once students and parents have seen first-hand just what a enjoyable experience a recital can be, they will agree to take part the next year.

Once the teacher has an accurate count of the number of students that will be performing, he or she should find out how many friends and relatives will also want to attend so that the size of the recital room can be determined and selected. A simple questionnaire often works well in this area.

For those teachers with just a few students, a living room may work exceptionally well, producing an atmosphere that is cozy and intimate. For those teachers with considerably more students, a larger area must be found that is conducive to running a recital and that will handle a greater number of people. Keep in mind that a recital does not have to be held in a large concert hall; it could be held in a church basement, a school auditorium, or any other large room that has a piano and adequate seating. If the room or hall does not have a piano, one may have to be rented or brought in for the day.

Once a place to run the recital has been found, teachers must make sure that the piano available for the performances is in tune and working properly. It would be quite embarrassing to come to the day of the recital only to find that the piano is unplayable or severely out of tune. Additionally, teachers will need to decide if any amplification equipment is needed.

Next, teachers should print programs listing the student's names, ages, how long they have been taking lessons, and the pieces that are being performed. Students should perform in age order, not in order of how long they have been studying. Otherwise, older students might end up following younger students, or vice-versa. The differences in ages would be intimidating, thus hindering the recital experience.

At the start of the recital the teacher should greet the guests. And, before each performance, the teacher should also introduce the student and give a quick synopsis of the piece being played. Another nice touch is for teachers to find something positive to say about each student and the progress he or she has made during the year.

Again, advance preparation will help students perform to the best of their abilities at a recital. Little things such as sitting correctly at the piano could easily affect a student's performance. In addition to sitting properly at the piano, students should practice their recital piece (or pieces) starting at various points. It is quite easy for students to suddenly draw a blank when performing at a recital. If they know they can jump to or continue from the nearest section, disaster can often be averted.

Once students have completed their performances, they should bow or curtsy before walking back to their seats. Teachers can seat all participants together or allow them to sit with their families. Either way seems to work equally well, unless, of course, there are so many participants that there is no other option than seating them together; teachers would not want to wait an exorbitant amount of time for students to make their way to the piano every time a name is called.

It is often advantageous for teachers, as well, to prepare a piece that they will perform at the end of the recital. There is nothing wrong with "showing-off" a little and setting the standard of performance. Added respect is gained by performing a musical composition of sufficient difficulty in front of parents and relatives. Of course, if you are more "teacher" than you are pianist, you do not have to make a fool of yourself by trying to perform a piece in public that is beyond your abilities; it is not imperative that you perform.

The dress code should be semi-formal. In other words, boys should be in jackets and ties and girls should be in dresses. Allowing students to perform in street clothes and jeans degrades the recital experience. This is a special day; students should dress appropriately. Of course, if boys do not have a sport's jacket or suit, they should not be forced to go out a buy one. In such cases, one can often be borrowed from a friend, or if that is impossible, boys should at least be required to wear a tie.

Once the recital is completed, participation certificates should be handed out along with a special recital gift. A musical pin or other inexpensive gift is a nice way of saying, "Thanks for a job well done!" By informing students and parents at the beginning of the recital that all award certificates and gifts will be handed out at the end of the recital, students and parents will be forced to remain for the entire program. Before implementing this procedure, the number of students, parents, and relatives that would walk out once their child had performed was shocking. One of the most important reasons for running the recital in the first place was to give students a perspective as to where they stood in relation to their peers. By leaving early, a valuable motivational tool was lost.

Another nice touch is for teachers to provide coffee and refreshments once the recital is completed. It is totally up to the discretion of the teacher as to how elaborate a spread he or she wants to have. But, remember it is better to have too much than too little.

Now we come to the decision of whether or not to charge a recital fee. If the cost of renting a hall, piano, chairs, printing programs and purchasing refreshments becomes prohibitive, then there is nothing wrong with charging a recital fee or selling tickets to offset expenses. Few parents would expect teachers to absorb the entire cost of producing a recital alone. However, if you are able to keep the costs low, you may want to forego the added fee.

One last note: If at all possible try to find a way of videotaping the recital. Parents that do not have video or digital cameras will be pleased to know that they can get a copy of the performances from you. However, make sure you only lend out copies, not originals; originals have a way of getting lost or ruined. Videotapes can be wonderful tools for teachers to evaluate and review performances. And, you will be able to cherish the moments for years to come.

Chapter Summary

Extrinsic motivation has little or no value in developing long-term motivation. Intrinsic motivation, or motivation from within, is produced as teachers find ways of building students' self-esteem through successful achievement at the piano.

The warmth and caring of the teacher is another highly motivational influence on students. Progress will occur at optimal rates when teachers take the time to build solid professional relationships with their students.

Praise must be used properly. Too much praise is just as unhealthy as too little praise. Praise should only be offered for achievements that are in line with students' abilities. Teachers must always be encouraging.

Recitals allow students and teachers a chance for self-evaluation, and thus can be highly motivational tools. Students should be prepared properly for recitals, but undue emphasis should not be placed on the recital piece. The lesson plan must stay intact at all times.

Teachers must take care to plan recitals adequately. With a little forethought and preparation the recital experience can be a positive one for all involved.

Next Chapter: What to Do When a Student Wants to Quit.

Chapter VIII-What to Do When a Student Wants to Quit

Teachers often consider it a personal failure when students decide to discontinue their musical training. But, the fact is that no matter how proficient one becomes at teaching, how caring and devoted, how innovative, etc, no teacher will be successful with every student all of the time. Yet, if sound teaching principles and techniques are carefully followed and applied, the incidences of student failure will decrease dramatically.

What is a teacher to do when a student wants to quit? Does the teacher A) shake the student's hand and wish him or her well; or, B) fight to keep the student from making a life-long mistake?

As you may have already guessed, the correct answer is B) fight to keep the student from making a life-long mistake. Obviously, the term "fight" is used in the sense of not easily letting go or working hard to identify the reasons leading to such a drastic action, rather than the use of verbal or physical abuse. Sometimes the extra effort on the part of the teacher is all that is needed to prove to students that the teacher is in truth committed to their musical growth.

At the onset of lessons it should be mentioned to parents that children are sure to experience the normal highs and lows when learning piano, as with anything else of great difficulty. When new and challenging material is presented, students will often experience acute frustration and seek to suspend instruction. Parents must expect these inevitable ups and downs and understand that through perseverance children build character. Students do not really want to quit; they only want the frustration to go away. However, if the requests to discontinue training persist week after week, then it cannot be assumed that immaturity is speaking, but that a serious problem exists, one that must be dealt with immediately.

The first thing that teachers should do when students seek to stop lessons is to find out the underlying reasons for such an action. Teachers should not accept superficial explanations as fact; rather, they should try to get to the root cause. Once the root cause has been determined, a meaningful discussion can be initiated where problems are dealt with and corrected.

If the student has simply lost interest in learning piano, then the teacher must evaluate his or her teaching methods and decide honestly whether or not sound pedagogical principles have been followed or if there is an area that is lacking. The vast majority of times students lose interest are because teachers have been unable to make the learning experience fun and exciting. Yet, teachers cannot always be held responsible for a student's failure. Often, there are numerous other factors that lead to a student's musical dysfunction.

The four most prevalent reasons why students seek to discontinue lessons are 1) chronic frustration caused by inconsistent practice; 2) excess parental pressure to succeed; 3) family crises or temporary conditions; and 4) hurtful comments made by the teacher or parents.

Overcoming Causes of Chronic Frustration

No one likes to be frustrated; and students are no different! Yet, chronic frustration in music usually comes as a result of inconsistent practice. The number one reason for inconsistent practice is student over-commitment.

Student over-commitment is all too pervasive in our society to-day. When speaking to parents about setting up a regular practice routine for their children, I often hear the same themes verbalized: "My child has two to three hours of homework each night. On weekends we're always running to soccer practice or gymnastics or swimming lessons, etc." The list of excuses goes on and on.

We have all heard the saying "jack of all trades, master of none." Well-intentioned parents often commit their children to such a wide variety of activities that it is impossible for any one to be excelled at. Children of such parents often drift from activity to activity; when one becomes too difficult, it simply gets dropped in favor of the next.

Sometimes this over-commitment is due to the fact that both parents work full-time and thereby try to compensate for the lack of time spent with their children. Unfortunately, greater and more sophisticated diversions do not make up for the lack of positive interaction with children.

I am not trying to insinuate that many families do not legitimately need two incomes to survive. I am only saying that when both parents work full-time, guilt often plays a role in student over-commitment. When students are pulled in too many directions, there is no way that a consistent practice routine can be achieved.

Should it become evident that a student is not giving piano his or her best, the teacher must determine if over-commitment is the culprit and deal with it head on. Activities that have little, if any, lasting benefits should be dropped in favor of those that do. Even when over-commitment is not the source of a student's frustration, teachers may find that there are other mindless activities that rob students of valuable practice time. Yes, children only get one chance at enjoying a childhood, but they do need to be prepared for adulthood. If the many hours of television and computer games were reduced by just one half-hour to an hour per day and replaced by consistent piano practice, virtually every student would be able learn to play proficiently and experience a lifetime filled with musical enjoyment.

Human beings are creatures of habit. Therefore, finding a consistent practice time is imperative if students are to succeed at the piano. But, where should piano practicing fit in the student's schedule? If practicing is done after homework is completed, the result will likely be students who are exhausted and in no mood to work diligently. On the other hand, if the practicing does get done first, most students will still find ways of completing their homework in a timely manner.

What worked for my children was to get up an extra half-hour early so that piano practicing could be done *before* school. At first I encountered a good amount of resistance to the idea. But after a while, once the activity became part of the daily routine, my children were actually glad to know that when they got home from a long day of school their practicing was already completed. Practicing before school may not work for every family, but if it can be implemented, it will solve a great many problems.

Another alternative is to tie piano practicing into a certain time slot. In other words, practicing might be scheduled immediately after school or before or after dinner, etc. The problem with the after-school time is that older children often make play dates and thus their minds will usually be somewhere else, such as at their friend's house, the park, or on the ball field, etc. Therefore, it is not generally a good idea to schedule practice time when students will be unable to concentrate or be focused.

It is not so much the time that is chosen, as it is the routine that is established. Routine is the key to consistent practice. One rule that should always be enforced is that students should never be allowed to watch TV, play computer games, carry on on-line conversations, etc, until all piano practicing and homework has been completed. Parents must not allow this rule to be broken. The old adage, "Give them an inch and they will take a foot" will surely come back to haunt any parent that capitulates in this area!

There are probably countless causes of frustration. However, if teachers are willing to get to the true source of the problem, then suggestions can be offered and problems can get corrected. Chronic problems must be dealt with and teachers must care enough to help students and parents rectify difficulties as they occur; they cannot give up too easily on their students!

Dealing with Excess Parental Pressure to Succeed

Just as when a teacher corrupts the learning experience by putting undue emphasis on worldly success, so will excess parental pressure lead students to feel contempt toward their instrument. When students get to the point where they have had enough, where music is not an area that they want to pursue in their lives any longer, there is almost no way of getting them back. Therefore, it is essential that the signs of excess parental pressure be recognized and addressed before the results become irreversible.

How does a teacher learn to recognize the warning signs of excess parental pressure? Simply by being alert! Of course, teachers are not usually present during the weekly practice sessions, but they can observe interactions between student and parent at the lesson; these exchanges can be most revealing. Is there a harsh tone to the parent's comments? Does the student wince every time his or her parent interjects? Does the student generally have a good attitude at the lesson and does he or she come in with an air of excitement?

These questions reveal the telltale sign of what is going on beneath the surface. When a teacher senses that something is not right, the problem must be dealt with before it gets past the point of no return. Some parents need to be reminded that if their children truly develop a love for the instrument, that intrinsic motivation will develop which will enable them to reach their full potential. However, not every student is destined to become a world-famous concert pianist; *but* virtually every student can learn to play to varying degrees of proficiency.

In cases where there are signs of undue pressure, teachers should take parents aside and talk privately. However, a one-minute conversation while the next student is waiting is not a professional way of handling a sensitive issue. Before any conference is held with the parents, though, it is not unreasonable to take a few minutes at the end of a lesson to tactfully question the student in private. As long as teachers act quickly, responsibly, and professionally, most areas of difficulty can be corrected long before students are permanently affected.

Handling Family Crises or Temporary Conditions

During the formative years there will be those times when a family crisis or temporary condition will prevent students from experiencing sustained progress on their instrument. If the problems are short-lived, then only a temporary dip in the Student Progress Graph will be noticeable. However, if the condition persists, then students will often seek to suspend lessons until such time as the situation is resolved.

As a general rule, it is not advisable for students to stop lessons during these periods of time. Once a student stops, the chances are great that he or she will never resume again. As time goes on and skills start to deteriorate, students are often embarrassed by how much they have lost; many times they will not want to recommence lessons for fear that their teacher and parents will be disappointed in them.

When a situation arises that has a high probability of being only temporary, teachers should demonstrate sincere concern and suggest to parents that students take their lessons anyway. Personal Scores as plotted on the Student Progress Graph could be suspended for a short period of time, as they would not have any real meaning. Students can be instructed to do whatever is possible during the week with the lesson merely acting as a review. This way the pressure to perform is removed and skills are not allowed to atrophy.

For those parents that are not enthralled with the idea of paying for lessons where their children will not be progressing, teachers must help parents understand that in this case standing still is better than falling backwards. If students stop lessons completely, they will surely take many steps back.

Also, parents must recognize the quandary that the teacher is put in: What is a teacher supposed to do, hold a time slot open indefinitely for a student that may or may not return? Many teachers have a list of students just waiting to be fit into their schedule once a spot opens up. It would be unfair to both teacher and potential student if an available time slot could not be filled. And, once a spot is filled, it becomes unavailable should that student wish to return at a later time.

Therefore, when any family crisis or temporary condition occurs, teachers should be understanding, but firm in their resolve to keep students continuing in their musical training. It is truly best for all parties involved. However, if parents insist on stopping lessons without a commitment date to resume, teachers should gently explain that the current time slot could not be guaranteed should they decide to recommence instruction at a later date. There is nothing wrong with doing everything in your power to keep the spot open, but it must be clear that there may be no other choice than to give it to a ready, willing, and able student.

Hurtful Comments Made by Teachers or Parents

What many teachers and parents do not realize is just how sensitive most children are; it does not take much for an adult to crush the spirit of a young person. What teachers and parents also do not appreciate is that the material that is so easy for them to comprehend is not always as easy for children to grasp. Therefore, even if teachers and parents do not come out and say it, the tone of their voice often leads children to believe that they must be stupid if they have any trouble understanding what is being taught.

To overcome this potential for disaster, teachers must guard their tone of voice and observe their students' countenance during the lesson. If facial expressions reveal that a student is upset, the teacher must deal with the child's emotional self before attempting to instruct the intellect. Under no circumstances should derogatory comments ever come spewing out of the mouth of a teacher or parent. Also, teachers must be careful not to have any rolling of the eyes or give any clue that they are exasperated by the student's lack of understanding. To the contrary, it is often advisable to preface any new material with words such as, "Now we come to a very difficult area," or, "This next section is extremely difficult, so if you have any questions I want you to feel free to ask." By putting themselves in the students' shoes, teachers send a message that the learning process will be faced together; that there is nothing too difficult that cannot be overcome.

Once a teacher crushes a student's spirit, there is no other recourse but to apologize. Excuses will not cut it; only the words, "I am so sorry, will you please forgive me" will correct the situation. Otherwise, the student's attitude will change and eventually the student will be lost. I cannot overemphasize the fact that hurtful and derogatory comments as well as a demeaning tone of voice are absolutely incongruous with the building of students' self-esteem.

Chapter Summary

Teachers must not give up easily when students seek to discontinue lessons. The reasons for such actions must be identified and corrected.

If teachers find that their students often stop because of loss of interest, then they need to reevaluate their teaching methods and determine whether or not sound teaching principles are being followed.

Other than loss of interest, there are four main reasons why students fail at piano: chronic frustration due to inconsistent practice, excess parental pressure to achieve, temporary conditions where students are allowed to suspend instruction but never come back, and hurtful comments made by the parent or teacher.

Each cause of musical dysfunction must be identified and dealt with before the results become irreversible. If caught early, situations can be corrected and students can be put back on the road to steady progress.

Next Chapter: The Business of Piano Teaching.

Chapter IX-The Business of Piano Teaching

If teachers are to be successful financially they must learn to treat piano teaching as a business. In this chapter we will look at 1) the establishment of lesson fees, 2) the development of a make-up policy for missed lessons, 3) lesson lengths, 4) in-home vs. studio lessons, 5) the purchasing of books and materials, 6) the keeping of records, and 7) miscellaneous business necessities.

Since the focus of this book has been to train teachers in the area of individualized instruction, this chapter, as well, will be geared toward those teachers giving private rather than group lessons.

Lesson Fees

As mentioned back in chapter one, teachers must establish a fee for their services that is in keeping with their level of expertise and in line with those charged by other teachers in the vicinity. Prior to setting their remuneration, new teachers and even experienced ones new to a particular locale must take time to research the range of rates incumbent to the neighborhood. As they do so, they should be cognizant of the fact that a teacher's fee is often considered to be indicative of a teacher's skill.

When a teacher's fee is significantly lower than that of the competition, many parents mistakenly come to the conclusion that the teacher is not as skilled as other more expensive instructors and are reluctant to hire that teacher. And, if the teacher does secure any students, it is almost impossible for him or her to raise rates to reasonable levels within an acceptable amount of time; for in order to boost rates to reasonable levels, the teacher would have to increase fees by double or triple-digit percentages, something most parents would find completely unacceptable.

So, before you set a fee for your services, you must determine what other teachers in your area are charging. As you make initial queries, find out if your competitor's rates are based on private or group instruction, for lessons given in the student's home or at the teacher's studio; whether they are based on half-hour, forty-five minute, or hour lessons; and if they are paid weekly, monthly, or per contract agreement. Also, try to ascertain the teacher's credentials. Once you know these details, you will have a better idea of the fees that you can realistically ask.

If you decide to charge a fee that is lower than the going rate, just to get established, but do not want to get locked into introductory prices, it is advisable that at the onset of lessons you give parents a fee-increase schedule designed to bring your rates up to competitive levels over a two to three year period. This way parents will know in advance what they will be paying six months or a year down the line and will not stop lessons in an over-reaction to multiple rate hikes.

If confronted by parents as to why you would insist on hefty increases, you can simply tell them that the going rate in the area is significantly higher than your introductory rate, and once you have had a chance to prove yourself, you do not think it unreasonable to be paid fees closer to that of other teachers. Although parents will not like the prospect of higher lesson costs, this sort of approach will elicit the respect afforded better-known instructors.

Next, you must decide how you want your fees to be paid. Do you want to receive payments weekly, monthly, or on a quarterly, semi-annual, or annual contract-rate basis?

After years of experimentation and vacillation on this issue, I have come to the definite conclusion that monthly rates work best. If teachers charge on a weekly basis they will encounter a tendency on the part of many parents to cancel excessive numbers of lessons. If the child has the sniffles, parents cancel the lesson; if the child has to stay after school, the lesson gets cancelled; the list of cancellation excuses goes on and on. What took me years to realize is that when fees are paid weekly an incentive is built in for students to miss lessons—no lesson, no payment!

To compensate for all the missed lessons, teachers who charge on a weekly basis are forced to develop an elaborate make-up policy to recapture lost income or suffer financial loss (this is not to mention trying to keep students on track). The problem is that no matter what the make-up policy states, whether lessons are made up only if given twenty-four hours notice, or under other conditions, teachers are faced with either creating hard feelings or making-up large numbers of lessons. Every time a make-up lesson is given, it represents two time slots, one for the missed lesson and one for the make-up lesson.

To make monthly rates work, teachers must require that parents pay at the beginning of the month for the entire month of study. In return, parents should be told that by paying monthly there is no additional charge for five-week months. However, should the student be forced to miss a lesson, the extra lesson must be considered a make-up lesson; if no lessons are missed, the fifth lesson, when it occurs, is free of additional charge.

Five-week months occur only once every three months for each day of the week. Consequently, with merely one make-up scheduled during a three-month period, the number of missed lessons will be reduced dramatically as well as the number of make-up lessons the teacher is required to give.

But, many teachers may be thinking, "Why should I have to charge the same fee for five-week months as I do for four-week months? If the student has not missed any lessons, I end up giving a free lesson." This criticism would be valid if teachers did not take the extra lesson into account before they calculated their monthly rate.

For purposes of simplicity, to calculate the monthly rate we will use a weekly fee of $10.00 per week (we could have just as easily used a hundred or a thousand dollars). $10.00 times four weeks equal a monthly rate of $40 per month, right? Wrong! The extra lesson has not been figured in. Since the extra lesson occurs once every three months, an extra one-third of the weekly fee (in this case $3.33 per month) must be added into the monthly rate. This way every three months an additional $10 is recouped. If the student has not missed any lessons, the teacher is paid for his or her time. If the student has missed a lesson, the teacher is still paid for the time of giving the make-up. Either way, the teacher is paid for his or her time.

Now many will say, "How can I charge a monthly rate of $43.33?" Yes, I agree, that would be rather odd. Therefore, teachers should round the number up to the nearest five-dollar increment. When calculating a monthly rate, take the weekly fee you would like to receive, multiply it by 4.33, and then round up to the nearest five-dollar increment.

Suppose you would like to be paid $50 per lesson. If you multiply that figure by 4.33 you get a monthly rate of $216.50. Rounding that number up to the nearest five-dollars, the monthly rate you would actually charge would be $220 per month. You now have a fee that covers you for all fifth lesson months and has taken the incentive away from students to miss their lessons.

Another variation to the monthly rate is the quarterly, semi-annual, or yearly contract rate. The thinking behind quarterly, semi-annually, or yearly pricing is that parents would receive a discount for committing to longer periods of lessons. The negatives are that most parents are unwilling to commit to long contracts unless the discounts are very deep; and even if they do, teachers then have to budget themselves because they will be receiving fewer (although larger) payments per year.

Make-Up Policy

As inferred from the previous section, the make-up policy that the teacher establishes is conditional upon the frequency of payments requested. If fees are based on quarterly, semi-annual, or annual contracts, then no make-up lessons should be offered. If students do not miss any lessons, they get the best value for their dollar. If they miss many lessons, their price-per-lesson increases considerably.

Still, for those teachers that prefer to be paid weekly, criteria for making-up missed lessons or requiring payment must be clearly laid out for parents, right from the start. Keep in mind that whatever policy you ultimately decide upon must be fair both to parents and teacher and must be in written form. If it is too one-sided, or only given verbally, misunderstandings will occur and parents will end up taking their business elsewhere, even if they are generally pleased with the quality of the teaching their child has been receiving.

At the very least, teachers should be given twenty-four hour notice of cancellation for any make-up lessons to be given. Of course, in cases of true emergencies, the rules could get bent. Unfortunately, what many parents consider emergencies are far different than what most teachers would accept. Therefore, if you are going to bend the rules, make sure it is for legitimate reasons.

Also, make-up lessons should be limited to no more than one per month. Regrettably, many parents will feel that a one-make-up lesson per month policy is extremely stringent. What they fail to realize is that if every student missed only one lesson per month and expected a make-up, the task of arranging make-up times would become insurmountable for the teacher. For example, if a teacher has sixty students and each student misses only one lesson per month, the teacher is faced with the dilemma of finding sixty openings to make up sixty lessons or lose a tremendous amount of income. Again, the policy of monthly payments solves these problems.

Next, a policy must be established for teacher-missed lessons, vacations, and summers. Generally, teachers cannot expect parents to pay for teacher-missed lessons, whether they are due to sickness, vacation, or personal reasons. If teachers are going to expect payment for student-missed lessons, then they must be willing to credit students when *they* are forced to miss lessons. If the teacher asks to reschedule a lesson when he or she must cancel, then the teacher must be willing to do the same when students are forced to cancel. The same policy should hold true for both student and teacher.

How should vacations be handled? As long as parents inform teachers of pending vacations prior to the month of study, there is no reason why they should not receive a credit or make-up lesson for the missed time. For those students on a monthly basis, if only one week is missed, it should be covered by the fifth lesson policy. For those students on a quarterly or longer contract, vacations should not be an issue, as students are already receiving discounted rates. For students paying weekly, the problem of no lesson, no payment will always exist.

Summer vacations should be handled much like any other vacation; as long as the teacher is informed of the student's plans in advance, adjustments can be made accordingly. Whatever you do, try to encourage your students to continue through the summer; it is best for them and best for you. When it comes to summers, though, flexibility is the operative word!

Half-Hour, Forty-Five Minute, or Hour Lessons

The amount of time necessary for each lesson will be determined by two factors: 1) the working pace of the teacher, and 2) the level of advancement of each student.

Many teachers like to work slowly and methodically. Other teachers prefer to zip along at a quick but steady pace. Therefore, the pace that the teacher is comfortable working at will largely determine the length of the lesson. Students should receive lessons that are long enough to get through the majority of the assignments most of the time. Some teachers can work within a half-hour format; others will need an hour to accomplish the same goals. Each teacher must determine for himself or herself what lesson length works best.

As students progress, sooner or later the amount of time required to review the assignments at the lesson will need to be increased. When the teacher gets the sense that the current lesson length is fast becoming inadequate, parents should be advised that in the near future the time would need to be augmented and the fee adjusted accordingly. The more advance the warning, the better it will be for everyone involved: student, teacher, and parent.

Another thing to keep in mind as you decide whether to give half-hour, forty-five minute, or hour lessons, is that the longer the lesson, the longer the down-time when a student misses a lesson. It is one thing to get a half-hour break, it is quite another to lose several hours in a day.

In-Home Vs. Studio Lessons

Whenever possible it is preferable for teachers to give lessons in their own home or studio rather than at the student's home. But in order to do that, there must be a professional working environment. If you have little ones running around the house or other interruptions, you cannot expect students to take lessons where disruptions will occur. On the other hand, if you give the lessons in the student's home, you are almost sure to have the lesson time disturbed.

There are a number of other reasons why studio-based lessons work better for teachers than lessons given in the student's home. First of all, when lessons are given at the student's residence, teachers must develop a route that optimizes their travel time. Unfortunately, there will always be certain students that need lessons scheduled at particular times. Therefore, teachers will often have to increase their travel time and incur additional mileage just to accommodate their students. It is bad enough to have to absorb the extra expense of fuel and wear-and-tear on your car, not to mention the lost time for travel; it is quite another thing to have to increase those expenses and the associated downtime in order to fit the lesson into a student's schedule.

In addition, when teachers give in-home lessons rather than at their studio, *they* are responsible to get to the student on time. Should the weather slow the roads, or accidents occur, teachers will lose precious minutes, yet must still find a way of giving each student their allotted time. When lessons are given at the teacher's studio, the onus is the parent to be punctual or forfeit valuable lesson time; they are the ones that must deal with all the problems traveling presents.

Another reason why studio-based lessons work better for teachers comes in the area of student-missed lessons. If the teacher has arranged a route and even one student cancels, the entire teaching schedule must be adjusted. Moving lesson times around while driving is a dangerous task to say the least. When students are forced to miss a lesson given at the teacher's studio, the teacher has the option of catching up on much needed work or easily making a few calls to offer other students an earlier time-slot.

Whether giving lessons at the home or at their studio, teachers must schedule in buffer periods so that bathroom breaks, important calls, and so forth will not throw off the teaching agenda. Generally, people dislike waiting; buffer periods allow teachers to easily get back on schedule.

Another time-waster that many teachers fail to consider is that when lessons are given at the home, many parents have a tendency toward excessive chitchat. It is much harder for them to carry on long conversations when the next student is sitting patiently in the waiting room.

If lessons are given at the student's home, travel time must be included in the lesson fee. Is a teacher's time any less valuable just because he or she is driving rather than teaching? Of course not! Yet, few parents are willing to double the fee if it takes the teacher an extra half hour to get to their home and back.

So, as you can see, lessons given at the teacher's studio will work much better for teachers than those given at the student's home. To help parents see the value of studio-based lessons, teachers can stress the importance of a professional atmosphere, and may even consider investing in recording equipment or computer software to facilitate student progress. It would be very hard for parents to argue the benefits of in-home lessons when they cannot offer half of what is available at the teacher's studio.

The Purchasing of Books and Materials

The purchasing of books and materials for students is the responsibility of the parent. Yet, some teachers will offer to pickup materials in order to assure that the student's progress does not become impeded should parents find themselves unable to get to their local music store in a timely fashion. In addition to assuring continued progress, many music stores offer professional discounts to teachers; so the difference between the teacher's purchase price and the retail price that parents ultimately pay can provide teachers with additional income.

If your local music store is not too far away and you would like to offer this service, make sure that parents know the approximate price of the book or music aid, and that you expect payment upon delivery (say it nicely of course!) Otherwise, you may end up waiting several weeks for payment. (There is no need to tell them that you will be making a profit; it is none of their business.)

As a general rule, if parents are given proper notice of the purchase particulars, and they still keep the teacher waiting for reimbursement, then those parents should be required to purchase their own books the next time around. Obviously, only teachers can decide if it is worth the aggravation of constantly having to ask for the reimbursement of monies expended on the student's behalf. But, having to outlay your funds for any extended period of time and having to badger parents for payment cannot be worth the small profit it brings.

If you require that parents do the purchasing of all books and materials, make sure you provide them with a written list of what is needed. Otherwise, parents are apt to make unwarranted substitutions or simply get the wrong items. As far as the next-book-in-a-series is concerned, make sure that parents know far enough in advance when the book is likely to be needed. Sometimes books are temporarily out of stock and must be reordered. By giving parents enough warning and advising them that the book may have to be ordered, teachers can guarantee that it will be ready and waiting by the time the student has passed the previous one.

The Keeping of Records

The keeping of income records is not only necessary for tax purposes but is also a good idea from a business point of view. Should any discrepancies occur as to whether or not a lesson fee has been paid, accurate records kept by the teacher will help to settle the dispute.

Most office supply stores offer attendance record journals for teachers. Another option is to use a computer-oriented time-management program or simple spreadsheet. Whatever method you prefer, make sure you log in all lessons given and payments received. It is also a good idea to keep track of all mileage incurred in the course of giving lessons as well as any other business related expenses. A good accountant can offer wise counsel in this area.

Miscellaneous Business Necessities

Finally, we come to the peripheral items that reflect on the professionalism of a teacher. At a minimum, teachers should have business cards made up listing their name, profession (piano instructor), telephone numbers, etc. Letterheads, envelopes, memo pads, etc, also add nicely to the overall package.

It is also a good idea for teachers to keep a cellular phone or beeper with them at all times when they are out of the office or studio. Should a student have to cancel a lesson at the last minute, the teacher does not want to find this out as he or she knocks on the door of the student's house. Cell phone and beeper numbers should be listed clearly on the teacher's business card. This way there is no excuse for parents not to get in touch with the teacher when an emergency arises.

Chapter Summary

The establishment of a lesson fee that is in keeping with a teacher's level of expertise and in line with those charged in the area is essential if teachers are to be successful financially.

Monthly rates solve many of the problems associated with missed lessons and weekly payments.

Teachers must also develop a written make-up policy for student-missed as well as teacher-missed lessons. The policy must be fair to all involved if a long-term relationship is to grow.

The teacher's working pace and the level of advancement of the student should determine the amount of time necessary for each lesson.

Whenever possible, lessons should be given at the teacher's studio rather than at the student's home. A professional working environment facilitates student progress.

The purchasing of books and materials is the parent's responsibility. However, teachers that provide this service should be compensated and reimbursed quickly.

Teachers must keep accurate attendance, as well as income and expense records.

Teachers will add to their degree of professionalism through business cards, letterheads, and so forth. Beeper and/or cellular phones numbers should be clearly listed on all business cards so that parents can contact teachers in cases of emergency.

Next Chapter: Final Comments and Insights.

Chapter X-Final Comments and Insights

In this book, the instruction to teachers has at times been fairly specific and at other times quite general. The reason for this is to make sure that teachers are not tempted to copy a specific style of teaching, but rather, are allowed to find ways of applying the principles contained herein to their own individual manner of teaching. In that light, this final chapter is written as a compilation of comments and insights designed to increase the teacher's overall effectiveness.

Different Students-Different Approaches

Every student is different. Therefore, the approach that teachers take should be different for each student. The standards must remain the same, but the way the teacher empowers the student to do his or her best must be adjusted to each student's unique personality.

Some children need a firm touch at the lesson; others need a teacher that is easygoing. Some children only respond to a teacher that is stern. Other children are completely intimidated by a teacher that seems cross.

Early on in the student's training the teacher must make an assessment as to what approach will get the student to do his or her best. And, this methodology may need to be adjusted, as student and teacher get more and more familiar with one other.

Teachers must always maintain a healthy distance between themselves and their students. I am not talking about physical distance; I am talking about the respect due a person in a position of authority or leadership. Teachers do not need to become best friends with their students. There should always be caring and concern; but students must know that at the lesson they must answer to the teacher. Students and teachers are not on equal terms; yet students and teachers can have fun together as they discover all that learning has to offer. So, teachers must endeavor to arrive at a balance that keeps the student pressing on toward the desired goals, at his or her optimal speed, while enjoying the lesson and the interaction with the teacher.

Setting the Standards

Teachers often struggle with the level of mastery that students must attain on each assignment. The standard should be set at 100% perfect. Anything less sends out the message that human perfection is not something to be strived for. Of course, there will always be those students that will not consistently reach this goal. In such cases, once a student's reasonable best has been achieved, it is better to move on to the next piece than to allow stagnation to occur. But, do be careful; students that are written off early as merely marginal often come back to surprise their teachers.

Reviewing Pieces at the Lesson

When listening to a piece for the first time at the lesson, teachers should allow students to play it through at least one time completely before interrupting and correcting any errors. It is quite exasperating to work on a piece for an entire week and then not even get the chance to play it once for the teacher without being stopped.

After the initial run-through, teachers should try to find something positive to say about the performance and then ask the student to play it once again. They can inform the student that during the second time through they will want to stop at the areas that need to be corrected.

Even if a student does play a piece well the first time through, it is a good idea for the teacher to hear it a second time anyway: to compare performances and to make sure that mistakes do not occur. The teacher can say something to the effect, "That was excellent, too good to hear only once, would you mind playing it again?" Most students will be only too happy to comply!

Wherever repeated mistakes occur, teachers should circle the areas on the page using pencil (or erasable pen) so that students will be reminded not to make the same mistakes as they practice during the week. But, as you review pieces with students, do not be too quick to point out errors; allow students the opportunity to correct a mistake before bringing it to their attention.

As mentioned in a previous chapter, demonstrating pieces sometimes helps students gain a better perspective as to what the teacher expects. If you do play selected passages for your students, make sure they read along with you. Do not be afraid to stop in the middle and ask the question, "Where am I on the page?" Demonstrations are always more effective when students stay alert!

There are minor mistakes and there are major mistakes. Minor mistakes may take the form of one-time missed notes or fingerings and so forth; major mistakes could be repeatedly missed rhythms, accidentals, key signatures, etc. When a specific mistake occurs over and over again at a lesson, and is identified by the teacher and subsequently corrected by the student, the entire piece should be reassigned for another week, even if the student is able to play the piece perfectly as a result of the correction. Just because a piece can be played perfectly after being corrected does not mean that the student has truly grasped the reason for his or her error. Major mistakes need an additional week of practice before the root cause is truly understood and internalized. Minor mistakes corrected easily at the lesson do not warrant an extra week of practice.

Fingerings

Poor fingerings are often the cause of mistakes. Many editors take great pains to write in fingerings that will enable students to perform pieces easily. Therefore, teachers should make sure that students use proper fingerings at all times.

As students become more advanced, they will oftentimes be able to come up with alternate fingerings that work. However, the fact is that most beginning students are not able to do this. Teachers must see that students get into good habits right from the start. Correct fingerings are essential to proper musical growth.

If time permits at a lesson, teachers might even discuss with students how an editor arrived at a particular fingering. Looking at the high and low points of a phrase can often give great insight as to why one fingering is superior to another. The more students understand, the more they will be able to apply that understanding to new and more difficult situations.

Writing the Assignment into the Practice Chart

When writing the next week's assignment into the student's practice chart, consider using a form of short hand to speed things up. For example "WIFS 2X Perf" could stand for "Write in the Fastest Speed done two times perfectly," or "1 NPB" could take the place of "One note-per-beat." "HT" and "HS" could stand for "Hands Together" and "Hands Separately." Of course, teachers will have to explain to students (and parents) exactly what the various short hand notations mean; for the writing of the assignments uses up valuable lesson time. Once everyone understands the teacher's notations, the business of reviewing the lesson can take precedent over the necessity of writing it down.

Also, when assigning a piece, the more difficult criteria should be practiced at least two times perfectly each day, not just once. Repetition and reinforcement are the keys to successful practice.

Looking at Hands

Make sure students do not look at their hands when playing musical compositions. If you catch them continually glancing down, take their assignment book and hold it above their hands to obstruct their view. Without saying a word you will have blocked the students' line of sight forcing them to look back at the written page. If they still do not look at the music, you can say, "Eyes on the music please!" Pieces should not be passed if students can only play them while looking down at their hands.

Regarding Memorization

Students should be exhorted not to memorize pieces at interim stages. Memorization should only take place after a piece has been perfectly mastered; then it can be memorized in sections, if necessary. Students often use "memorization" as an excuse to look down at their hands, not the music!

Keep it Light

Chuckle when small mistakes occur; use humor. In other words, have fun at the lesson. But, at the same time, do not fool around; a great deal of work has to be covered in a short period of time.

Righteous Indignation

It is okay to get upset with students when they make up excuses or lead you to believe that they have tried their best when they obviously have not. If you are absolutely sure the assignment could have been mastered given a reasonable amount of effort, then make sure your students understand your displeasure. However, under no circumstances should students ever be yelled at or talked down to.

Taking Over a Student from another Teacher

When taking over a student from another teacher, you must find out what the student knows and what he or she does not know. This can be a time-consuming process. It is often a good idea to explain to the student that it may take several months for you to get him or her on a program that will plug the holes in the learning process and allow steady progress to be made. But, you must get that student onto a program that *you* are comfortable with, even if it is one step at a time.

Two mistakes that teachers often make when taking over a student from another teacher: 1) they keep the student on the same program used by the former teacher, a program that they are neither familiar with nor comfortable with. 2) They immediately switch the student over to the new books and materials, thus unnecessarily disrupting the learning process.

Both extremes are unnecessary; a gradual process is much wiser. As the teacher gets to know the student, and his or her strengths and weaknesses, the teacher can establish a plan that will allow him or her to move ahead step by step. Taking over other teacher's students is not an easy task. But, if approached systematically, the transition can be handled without too much difficulty.

Final Salutation

Embarking on a career in piano teaching is an exciting adventure to say the least. Few other vocations allow one individual to become instrumental in the life of another as does teaching piano. Therefore, teachers must take their chosen profession seriously, realizing that their skill and caring could easily be the difference between a student ever learning to play or not.

Teachers must treat their teaching as if they were creating a work of art, with each student representing a possible masterpiece.

May God bless you as you endeavor to build the self-esteem of your students through the learning of piano.

About the Author

Born in 1954 in Syosset, New York, Dino P. Ascari started taking piano lessons at the age of five. At thirteen he began teaching and performing professionally.

In 1976 Dino received a B.A. degree from Stony Brook University, majoring in music. The following year, he completed a Master of Science degree in Music Education from Long Island University and became Director of Teacher Development at the Malverne School of Music on Long Island.

In 1997 Dino and his wife Deborah became published songwriters placing their song, "You Are the One I've Waited For" on the Toni Walker CD, "Making Christ Known."

Currently residing with their four children in Melville, New York, Dino's commitment to excellence in the field of piano pedagogy has, to date, spanned over thirty-five years. Dino P. Ascari is a member of the Music Teachers National Association (MTNA).

Printed in the United States
1539900005B/184-189